TRUTH AT WORK

WITHDRAWN

TRUTH AT WORK

The Science of Delivering Tough Messages

MARK MURPHY

Mc
Graw
Hill
Education

New York   Chicago   San Francisco
Athens   London   Madrid   Mexico City
Milan   New Delhi   Singapore   Sydney   Toronto

1 2 3 4 5 6 7 8 9   LCR   22 21 20 19 18 17

ISBN   978-1-260-01185-2
MHID   1-260-01185-2

e-ISBN   978-1-260-01186-9
e-MHID   1-260-01186-0

This publication is designed to provide accurate and authoritative information in regard to the subject matter covered. It is sold with the understanding that neither the author nor the publisher is engaged in rendering legal, accounting, securities trading, or other professional services. If legal advice or other expert assistance is required, the services of a competent professional person should be sought.

—From a Declaration of Principles Jointly Adopted
by a Committee of the American Bar Association
and a Committee of Publishers and Associations

McGraw-Hill Education books are available at special quantity discounts to use as premiums and sales promotions or for use in corporate training programs. To contact a representative, please visit the Contact Us pages at www.mhprofessional.com.

To Andrea, Isabella, and Andrew

CONTENTS

ACKNOWLEDGMENTS

I hate to be cliché, but there really are too many people to thank individually for making contributions to this book. My researchers and trainers, and each of our hundreds of fantastic clients, deserve a special thank you. This book, and the research behind it, wouldn't exist without all of their efforts.

I would also like to highlight a few individuals who made special contributions to this particular book.

Andrea Burgio-Murphy, PhD, is a world-class clinical psychologist, my wife and partner through life, and my creative sounding board. Since we started dating in high school, I have learned something from her every single day. My children, Isabella and Andrew, daily reinvigorate my faith in the future of humanity. They are truly my inspiration.

Lyn Adler has worked with me for more than a decade. She is my personal editor and a brilliant thinker. I am deeply indebted to and grateful to Lyn for her help. Lyn understands the content better than anyone I've ever had working with me, and as with all of my other books, Lyn's help made this one possible.

Jill Sutherland is the newest member of our team, but she has taken on tremendous operational responsibilities and performed them brilliantly. Jill has kept the trains running on time better than anyone I've ever had working with me.

Mark Fortier is my publicist, strategist, and friend. His insights and guidance have always been exceptionally helpful and valuable. The editorial team at McGraw-Hill Education, especially Cheryl Ringer and Donya Dickerson, deserves a very special thank you for recognizing the need for this book and making the process fast and smooth.

Finally, I'm very lucky to have the guidance of numerous impressively smart people, including Troy Palmer, Paul Wakeman, Jonathan Wilson, Alba Alemán, John Sheehan, Dennis Hoffman, Joanne Hovis, Rick Haig, Richard Humphrey, Tony Pfister, Anthony Nievera, Kevin Andrews, Phil Rubin, Ned Fitch, and Tom Greenwood.

For More Information

For free downloadable resources including quizzes and discussion guides, please visit www.leadershipiq.com/truth.

INTRODUCTION

Have you ever found yourself in a conversation with someone who just couldn't or wouldn't hear the truth, no matter how many different ways you tried to explain it? Have you ever felt frustrated because you couldn't tell an employee, spouse, boss, neighbor, or coworker what you were really thinking? Have you ever avoided giving feedback to an employee, held back from correcting your boss, or abstained from disagreeing with a colleague? Or have you had one or more of these difficult conversations and the person reacted so badly that you regretted saying anything?

HAS THIS HAPPENED TO YOU?

Take a look at the following situations. Do any of them sound familiar to you?

My Feedback Goes Ignored

Taylor manages the tech support department, and one of her employees hasn't been filling out his programming requests correctly. So she stops by his desk and says, "Hey Hunter, I noticed you're not filling out the error logs in your programming requests. We need to do that for reporting purposes. Can you take a look at your requests?" Hunter replies, "Oh, yeah, I keep forgetting about it; sorry. I'll update my open ones. I'll try to keep it in mind." Taylor says thanks and walks away.

A week later nothing has been fixed, so Taylor stops by Hunter's desk and once again says, "Hey Hunter, I noticed you're not filling out the error logs in your programming requests. We need to do that for reporting purposes. Can you take a look at your requests?" This time Hunter huffily replies, "These rules change all the time. How do

1

you expect us to keep up? Like I've got nothing else to do but random data entry, just because the programmers can't look up the error logs themselves. But okay, fine. I guess I'll put all my real work on hold for the afternoon so I can report on work that's already done."

The Boss Dodges My Calls

Frank is part of a pilot project allowing select employees to work from home three days a week. Frank's been happier, more productive, and working longer hours. But he still needs input from his boss to finish some projects, and that's where he's having a problem. While the boss espouses a strong commitment for Frank's ability to work from home, on telecommuting days he doesn't respond to Frank's calls. Even Frank's e-mails can go unanswered. And this avoidance is causing Frank to miss deadlines and customers to get angry.

Frank tried to have a face-to-face with the boss about this, but the boss just says, "There's no problem, Frank. I have lots of work and I get busy, too, you know." Other employees have told Frank that the boss has a wicked passive-aggressive streak with a dose of vindictiveness. And now Frank's worried that if he keeps telecommuting, his career at this company is over.

I Was Attacked on Social Media

Karen's Facebook friends are pretty similar to her politically, so much of the time her feed contains articles that she's inclined to like. But on a Friday morning she sees that someone has posted an article that is just filled with misinformation, lies, and slander. Normally she'd just ignore it, but she can't let this garbage go uncontested. She writes a detailed debunking of the article expecting thanks for her analysis. Instead, over the next few hours she receives a steady stream of vitriol, unfriending, and even one person uninviting her to a party.

My Coworkers Are Jealous

Sam joined the hospital as a researcher a few months ago. Sam's boss hailed the hiring as the "coup of the decade," which, predictably, led to some resentment and jealousy from the other researchers. While no one has explicitly told Sam, "I don't like you," one coworker in particular has been pretty sarcastic and flippant when answering Sam's questions. Just the other day, when Sam asked this person a simple question about which policy to use for a new project, he replied, "Oh, Einstein needs help from the little people? Should I fetch you a latte while I'm at it?"

My Spouse and I Are on Different Wavelengths

Jane came home from work after a 12-hour day and plopped into her favorite chair only to have her husband, Bill, bound into the room and say, "Hey, you'd better get ready; my parents are gonna be here in 30 minutes!"

Stunned, Jane says, "What? You never told me they were coming over!"

"I'm pretty sure I mentioned it," says Bill. "Plus you've been so tired from work, you probably just forgot . . . again."

Jane knows Bill never mentioned his parents' visit, and this is the fourth time something similar has happened in the past few months. She's had several talks with him about it, and each time he denies any wrongdoing and, worse, blames her for forgetting.

Dealing with an Unappreciative Employee

CJ's feeling good about telling Stuart that he's getting a 5 percent raise. Who wouldn't want more money, right? But when he does the big reveal, Stuart just stares blankly, then frowns and says, "That seems low." CJ is dumbfounded. Stuart is one of the few employees even getting a raise, and 5 percent is on the higher end. And yet, he's griping that it's not enough? CJ's about to uncork when Stuart abruptly stands up, mumbles, "Thanks, I guess," and walks out the door.

My Great Idea Got Shunned

Eileen, a teacher, finds herself in yet another teacher meeting where the hot topic is the daily struggle to get students into the classroom and into their seats, attendance taken, and the class focused and working. After listening to 40 minutes of griping with no discussion of solutions, Eileen dares to share her creative idea with the group.

"Instead of sitting at our desk doing our own work while students wander into the classroom, let's stand outside the classroom door. We'll greet each student by name as we check the student's name off on the attendance roster and provide a short and simple message of positive expectation. And then the students will receive a numbered card that matches their new assigned seating and invites them to take a seat and get right to work on a 'Do Now' assignment posted on the board."

Eileen figures her peers will love this idea because it's inexpensive, easily implemented, low risk, and high reward. But instead, all she hears is "That won't work here," "I know my students would hate that," and "That seems like a lot of work."

What do all of these situations have in common? In every case, someone needed, or tried, to share some truth, and the other person or people resisted, avoided, blamed, lied, or denied.

GETTING PEOPLE TO HEAR THE TRUTH IS HARD

Most of us have encountered the frustration and difficulty of getting people to hear and understand the truth. Maybe you've got a brilliant idea that would improve your company but nobody will listen. Or you need certain employees to improve their performance but they won't accept that there's a problem. Maybe you're trying to get your coworkers to be more collaborative but they won't stop bickering and causing drama. Maybe your boss isn't supporting you or your spouse is lying to you. Maybe your customers are causing drama or your coworker is simultaneously brilliant and nasty. Whatever the particulars, we've all got situations where life would be so much better if we could just get people to hear the truth.

My firm recently surveyed nearly 10,000 employees and managers, and 9 out of 10 employees said that they've avoided confronting a coworker about inappropriate behavior, even when a customer or the organization suffered as a result.

One horror story left me shaken. A hospital nurse wrote to me that another nurse on her unit who was having trouble inserting IV lines attributed her difficulty to the gloves she wore. So after she put the gloves on, she would rip off two of the fingers so she could grip things (like IVs) more easily. And in case you're wondering, yes, that would absolutely defeat the purpose of wearing the gloves in the first place and endanger countless patients. The nurse who wrote me said that because the glove-ripper was an intimidating personality, "we all avoided saying anything to her for over a month."

The survey also found that 8 out of 10 managers have avoided confronting a subordinate about inappropriate behavior. This finding is especially bad given that this is a foundational piece of being a manager. What's the point of even having people in managerial roles if they're afraid to address an employee who's doing the job wrong or inappropriately or even dangerously?

And finally, perhaps the least surprising result was that nearly 9 out of 10 employees have avoided confronting their boss when he or she failed to fulfill an expectation or promise.

What's at the root of all these communication failures? According to our study, three out of four people say that the other party gets angry or defensive when they speak up about sensitive topics.

Some of the Greatest Names in History Had Problems Getting People to Hear the Truth

In the mid-nineteenth century, about 10 percent of women who gave birth in hospitals died. That's 1 in 10 mothers that died, most commonly from a gruesome and painful infection called childbed fever.

Fortunately, an obstetrician named Ignaz Semmelweis[1] worked at the famed Vienna General Hospital during this time. He noted that doctors and their students often began their days performing barehanded autopsies on the corpses of the previous day's victims of childbed fever. After the autopsies, the doctors would travel to the wards to examine women about to deliver babies.

If reading this makes you nauseous, it should. It's obvious today that doctors need to wash their hands in between autopsies and delivering babies (my kids could list hundreds of situations that necessitate hand washing). But the germ theory of infection didn't exist yet, leaving Dr. Semmelweis to postulate that childbed fever was caused by cadaveric particles adhering to the hands of the physician examining childbed patients.

He mandated that his medical students and junior physicians wash their hands in a chlorinated lime solution until the smell of the dissected bodies was gone. Immediately after his mandate took effect in 1847, the death rate of new mothers plummeted from 10 percent to 1 percent. Previously, 1 in 10 mothers died, and within a month, Dr. Semmelweis dropped that to 1 in 100.

It sounds like a fairly happy ending, right? Unfortunately, since this is a book partly about why people resist hearing the truth, our story doesn't end here. The doctor's discovery was overwhelmingly denied, resisted, or attacked, resulting in his dismissal from Vienna General Hospital. Ostracized, Dr. Semmelweis was forced to move from Vienna to Budapest.

His peers wrote articles attacking his idea. Carl Levy, a prominent Danish obstetrician, wrote, "I must judge provisionally that his opinions are not clear enough and his findings not exact enough to qualify as scientifically founded."

Dr. Semmelweis, who was not a particularly warm and fuzzy guy to begin with, was outraged by the attacks and his fellow obstetricians' indifference to the death of so many mothers. He wrote angry letters that denounced the obstetricians who ignored him as irresponsible murderers. Eventually people, including his wife, concluded that he was going crazy. In 1865 he was committed to an asylum where it's generally believed that he was severely beaten upon arrival by the guards. He died 14 days later.

We Need Truth Talks

A Truth Talk is a conversational process in which hard truths are shared, accepted, and embraced by your truth partner. More technically, a Truth Talk is a fact-based dialogic process that reduces the listener's psychological barriers to hearing, accepting, and acting upon hard truths.

Whether you're trying to gain acceptance for a brilliant discovery, convince an employee to get to work on time, stop your coworker from being a jerk, or urge your boss to tell you the truth about why she's mad, a Truth Talk makes hard truths easy to hear. A Truth Talk requires three elements.

First, the conversation must be based in fact. Truth Talks are not blurting out rumors, half-truths, and ill-considered opinions. Walking up to a coworker and shouting "You are so freakin' annoying!" is harassment, not truth. Facts are generally easy to accept; it's all the judgments and feelings that derail our conversations. And that means that before we open our mouths to initiate a Truth Talk, we have to exert some effort to distill and validate our message.

Second, the conversation should create change. Venting to scratch an emotional itch won't induce change. A Truth Talk requires asking, "Is what I'm about to say going to create change, or am I just blowing off steam without any real purpose?"

Third, the conversation is a dialogue, not a diatribe. People have a plethora of defenses with which to protect themselves from hearing hard truths. And hurling speeches at them is no way to circumvent those defenses. The only scientifically validated approach is to engage people in a true dialogue, such that they lower their own defenses and welcome the truths we have to share.

Each of us faces a ready supply of situations appropriate for Truth Talks. I recently surveyed more than 1,100 employees, and collectively they identified more than a dozen situations per day where having a Truth Talk would be beneficial. It doesn't matter if the recipient is your spouse, boss, employees, coworkers, customers, kids, kids' teachers, or neighbors; every day brings ample situations that require delivering tough messages.

THE WORLD WOULD BE BETTER WITH MORE TRUTH TALKS

The consequences of not having Truth Talks are calamitous. Businesses fail, employees fear for their jobs, managers worry about getting sued, teachers are afraid of getting shot, divorce rates remain high, and parents still can't find a way to communicate with their kids. Even our political disagreements have, in some cases, literally descended into violence.

Would you feel safe to speak the truth to your boss about an incompetent coworker or an impossible deadline? Or would you stay silent? In 2014, following the news of faulty ignition switches and a recall of millions of cars, GM CEO Mary Barra realized that far too many employees were staying silent. She announced a "Speak Up for Safety" program, saying "GM employees should raise safety concerns quickly and forcefully, and be recognized for doing so."[2]

Not that long ago, in 2007, Nokia produced more than half the planet's mobile phones, and its mobile operating system was on nearly two-thirds of the world's phones. Today it's easy to forget its name because by 2013 Nokia was crushed by Apple, Google, and Samsung. The once successful company's demise is superficially a story of strategic and technological mistakes. But a recent study from INSEAD researchers, involving 76 interviews with top and middle managers, engineers, and external experts, finds that Nokia was destroyed by "a culture of temperamental leaders and frightened middle managers scared of telling the truth." One middle manager interviewed describes how when a colleague suggested that he challenge a top manager's decision, "he didn't have the courage; he had a family and small children."

When Texas recently passed a law making it legal to carry concealed weapons into college and university buildings, including classrooms, the University of Houston's faculty senate suggested that professors should "drop certain topics from your curriculum" and "not 'go there' if you sense anger."

NASA is a classic example[3] of the dangers of failing to speak the truth. As Harvard Business School professor David Garvin explains, "If you think about the *Challenger* space shuttle explosion [in 1986], the incident was attributed to cultural issues: an unwillingness to speak up and accept dissonant voices. Then, seventeen years later, we have the *Columbia* explosion."

The list of organizations that have suffered for a lack of truth speaking is long and illustrious:[4]

- Detroit automakers didn't want to speak the truth about the marketplace surge of Japanese cars.

- IBM didn't want to speak the truth about Apple.
- American Airlines didn't want to speak the truth about cross-state rival Southwest Airlines.
- Kodak didn't want to speak the truth about digital photography.
- The music industry didn't want to speak the truth about MP3 file sharing.
- Michael Jackson's entourage didn't want to speak the truth about the pop star's drug dependence.

If you're a history buff, you can find ample examples of human inability to handle the truth dating back centuries. When the great astronomer Copernicus presented his heliocentric theory back in 1539, few people took him seriously that the earth circled around the sun. He was considered a heretic for speaking the truth.

A few decades later Galileo telescopically proved that Copernicus was speaking the truth. But popular belief and religious dogma didn't find it convenient to listen. Galileo was censured, was tried by the Inquisition and found "vehemently suspect of heresy," was forced to recant, and spent the rest of his life under house arrest. The Catholic Church finally took back the sentence in 1992.

Isaac Newton, who is widely recognized as one of the most influential scientists ever, made the majority of his discoveries before the age of 30, but it took him years to disclose those findings to the world. He feared that speaking the truth would make him a laughingstock to people who were generally superstitious and afraid of anything they didn't understand.

What if you're a high performer who can't tell your boss the truth about the shoddy performance of the low performers you work with? Or maybe you tried to have a Truth Talk but you were ignored or attacked? You wouldn't feel engaged and fulfilled. You'd probably feel unhappy. You might even feel outraged, like Dr. Semmelweis did.

In 2013, I published a study[5] with findings so counterintuitive that it captured media attention all the way from NPR to Rush Limbaugh. The study results showed that in nearly half of companies, low performers are happier than high performers. This news was shocking because it's not how things are supposed to work. If you're a high performer, you're supposed to be engaged and fulfilled and all the rest. And if you're a low performer, you're supposed to be miserable and disengaged.

But when you're a high performer who's getting stuck doing all the work because no one will listen to the truth about the low performers, you're likely to be miserable. It doesn't matter if you're Ignaz Semmelweis, Isaac Newton, or a high performer trying your best to do your job. Few things in life are more frustrating and demoralizing than trying to speak the truth and getting shot down, ignored, or attacked for the attempt.

When the *Wall Street Journal* covered the study,[6] it received over 200 online comments in the first day. And many of the comments followed the pattern of this one that said, "Things got so bad here we asked for a review from our corporate office HR department. They came and listened to our complaints and the lazy unproductive people had nothing bad to say. The productive hard workers had plenty to say and we asked to start making everyone accountable. It seemed like an easy request. Wrong. They did nothing. So the slackers are still slacking."

Failure to speak the truth doesn't just hurt us in the workplace. Over 70 percent of parents are afraid to talk to their kids about topics like drugs or sex. Likewise, husbands and wives regularly avoid difficult topics in order to skirt negative consequences and unproductive arguments filled with defensiveness and anger.

In the workplace, when employees don't feel comfortable speaking the truth to their boss, coworkers, or employees, they are more likely to consider quitting. And it's no better for bosses. Consider Joe, who got promoted to the position of manager instead of Ron, who had similar qualifications and experience.

Up until Joe's promotion, the team was forward focused and generally supportive of one another. But Ron didn't take kindly to getting passed over for the job. He built support with a faction of his peers who are committed to sabotaging Joe's success through actions like withholding critical information, shooting down Joe's ideas in meetings, starting rumors, and refusing to help or give advice. Everyone on the team silently acknowledges what is happening and how it is dividing the team, but Joe is afraid to speak the truth to Ron for fear that it will make things worse. No one's happy, and no one's talking.

The level of willingness to broach sensitive topics and to achieve understanding, not anger, is a valued measure of success for an organization's culture and its leaders. A culture of accountability can't exist when people won't engage in conversation about important topics. And far too many people suffer needlessly because employees and leaders can't, or won't, speak the truth.

THE TRUTH IS HARD TO HEAR, EVEN WHEN IT'S HELPFUL

Every day, smart, ostensibly rational people turn away from information that contradicts what they already believe. Take scientists, for example, and the case of *Helicobacter pylori* (*H. pylori*), a spiral-shaped bacterium found burrowed deeply in the gut of half the world's population. Thanks to the persistence of Dr. Barry Marshall,[7] we know today that *H. pylori* causes peptic ulcers. This knowledge allows us to easily treat the painful medical condition of peptic ulcers with antibiotics. But when Marshall proposed his theory back in 1982, he was met with overwhelming resistance.

His colleagues, who despite a lack of conclusive testing believed that stress and spicy foods caused ulcers, had no interest in listening to Marshall speak the truth. "I saw people who were almost dying from bleeding ulcers, and I knew all they needed was some antibiotics, but they weren't my patients," Marshall says. "To gastroenterologists, the concept of a germ causing ulcers was like saying that the Earth is flat."

Luckily, Marshall didn't give up. But he had to go to extremes, even experimenting on himself, to get his peers to listen. After "borrowing" a sample of *H. pylori* from the gut of an ailing patient, he swizzled the organisms around in a cloudy broth and drank it. A few days later he developed gastritis, the precursor to an ulcer: he started vomiting, his breath began to stink, and he felt sick and exhausted. Marshall biopsied his own gut, culturing *H. pylori*, and proved unequivocally that the bacteria were the underlying cause of ulcers. Still no one listened.

Marshall spoke the truth, sharing information that would benefit millions of people suffering from ulcers, but the medical establishment denied and even attacked this truth for decades.

Marshall did win the Nobel Prize for his work, 23 years after he slugged down that noxious bacterial cocktail. That's over two decades of human pain and suffering while supposedly smart, ostensibly rational gastroenterologists resisted the truth. Most of us don't have 23 years to wait. We need to speak the truth to our employees, colleagues, bosses, spouses, and children today.

THE ANATOMY OF A TRUTH TALK

This book will show you how to conduct a Truth Talk using an eight-step process, as follows.

Step 1: Understand the Truth-Killers (or Why We Resist the Truth)

The first step in any Truth Talk is getting familiar with the Truth-Killers. The latest research shows that people don't want to hear the truth. What they do want to hear is information that confirms their preexisting prejudices. And it's not enough to simply state the facts and hope that people will change their minds. Even in the face of indisputable truth, phenomena like cognitive dissonance, the Dunning-Kruger effect, and selective perception often cause people to deny, resist, or attack the truth. When you're about to enter a Truth Talk, it's a good idea to keep a mental checklist of the four Truth-Killers: Confident Unawareness, Psychological Resistance, Perceptual Resistance, and Financial Resistance.

Step 2: Focus on the Facts

Before you can start a Truth Talk, you've got to make sure you understand what the truth actually is. Every conversation has four layers: Facts, Interpretations, Reactions, and Ends (I call this the FIRE Model). In a Truth Talk, the easiest way to ensure that someone hears your tough message is to drop all the interpretations, reactions, and ends (the emotional and judgmental stuff) and just focus on the facts. By focusing on facts, you remove all the emotional baggage, judgment, and negative energy and free your truth partner to hear the truth.

Step 3: Take Their Perspective

Once you've distilled the facts, it's time to climb inside your truth partner's mind to see the situation from his or her perspective. Not only does this lower people's defensiveness, but when we understand their perspective, we can anticipate why they might be inclined to resist the truth. From here we can take steps to mitigate that resistance.

Step 4: Set Your Goals

Once you've clarified your facts and you understand your truth partner's perspective, it's time to assess what you can realistically achieve in your Truth Talk. If the facts are especially difficult, and your truth partner is experiencing one or more Truth-Killers, you may need to take a more staged approach to your Truth Talk. But before you set an effective goal for your Truth Talk, be sure you aren't setting one of the ineffective goals described in Chapter 4 that are certain to derail the conversation.

Step 5: Start a Conversation, Not a Confrontation

Have you ever tried to have a conversation with someone about something important, but the person just wouldn't listen? Sometimes people plug up their ears in defiance, or they mentally duck out of the conversation through denial, ignoring, evading, or lying. It's so frustrating, it can make you want to grab the person and shake your words into his or her brain. But confrontations don't work; they only invite resistance. The only surefire way to initiate change is to send a message that awakens a commitment from your truth partner. This is accomplished by using the IDEAS script.

Step 6: Create a Word Picture

When everyone has a different definition of the truth, an argument is virtually guaranteed. And far too many disagreements occur because we don't have a clear and shared definition of what the truth is. So we're going to create a Word Picture: a tripartite definition that transforms abstract concepts into concrete examples that anyone can understand.

Step 7: Listen with Structure

One of the critical skills you'll need to conduct a Truth Talk has nothing to do with talking; rather, it's all about listening. Once you've set your goals, begun a dialogue, and created a Word Picture, you're going to hit a point in the conversation where your truth partner will really start talking. This is when people share what's going on inside their head, reveal their interpretations, reactions, and ends, and basically tell you everything you should know to engage them effectively. The catch is that if you don't listen deeply, you'll never get any of that information. The process we're going to employ involves three parts: eliciting, listening, and confirming. Or what I call Structured Listening.

Step 8: Share the Facts

Before we start sharing our facts, we need to employee the FIRE Model and strip away all the interpretations, reactions, and ends. Then, when we're ready to share the facts, we're only going share enough to ensure that our truth partner makes a corrective leap. We need our truth partner to make a corrective leap because once that light bulb is on, we can then say, "Let's talk about how we can make things better in the future."

Far too many difficult conversations get stuck in looking backward, discussing ad nauseam all the things that went wrong. While we do need to look backward a bit to create a corrective leap, ideally we're going to spend the bulk of our time designing a better future.

Now that you know where we're going, let's get started.

1

UNDERSTAND THE TRUTH-KILLERS (OR WHY WE RESIST THE TRUTH)

Pat and Julian are salespeople for a software company. They'd been jointly working for five months to land a major account, and two weeks ago they conducted what they hoped would be the final sales presentation.

The pair got to the prospective client's office with time to spare and set up in the boardroom. The executives arrived, and the meeting seemed to proceed smoothly. But then, after an hour of answering detailed questions about the proposal, Pat's frustration boiled over. "I've gotta be honest," he told the client, "we've been working with you for three months answering all your questions, and this has reached the point of absurdity. Either go with us or don't, but we're done answering questions."

Julian's jaw dropped and his face went white as the prospective client's CEO said, "We won't be going with you," and walked out of the boardroom.

On the drive back to their office, Julian confronted Pat: "What were you thinking in there? We were about to close that deal and you give them an ultimatum like that? Seriously, what were you thinking?"

Pat shook his head and said, "You don't understand how business works, Julian. Sometimes you've gotta play hardball. And frankly, they would've been a pain to work with. I'm glad they're gone."

Over the next few days, Julian tried to get Pat to admit the truth about what happened in the meeting. But each time Pat dismissed him with "You're overreacting" or "You don't understand hardball sales" and even "I'm the most talented salesperson on the team, so I think I know what I'm doing." And with each rebuff, Julian's resolve to get Pat to admit his mistake strengthened. He even enlisted their manager to speak to Pat, but those comments also fell on deaf ears. Finally, an exasperated and desperate Julian asked, "Pat, is there any situation where you'd be willing to admit a mistake?"

"Nope," Pat replied, "because I don't make mistakes."

Julian felt like his head would explode. How could Pat be so resistant to accepting the truth that was so clear to everyone else?

THE TRUTH HURTS

Have you ever been in a conversation with someone like Pat who just couldn't, or wouldn't, hear the truth, no matter how many ways you tried to explain it? Or maybe you tried to tell somebody the truth and that person reacted so badly that you regretted saying anything at all.

Most people say yes when asked if they want to hear the truth. In fact, 88 percent of employees say they would want to hear the truth if their job performance was poor. And yet how many people do you know who, after slaving away on a big project, are grateful when the boss says, "That report you wrote was illogical, poorly written, two hours late, and riddled with typos"? I've witnessed adults who insist they can handle the truth cry, rant, and even punch the walls upon hearing truth like that.

The truth sounds good in theory, especially if it's truth with which we agree or that positions us in a favorable light. It's when we hear truth that isn't so pleasant that we start to resist. Pat didn't want to hear the unpleasant truth that he had botched a major deal. But I'm sure had things gone differently, if his ultimatum to the client had cinched the deal instead of losing it, he would have been delighted to hear that he'd saved the day and won the big contract.

In the conclusion of *Walden*, Henry David Thoreau summarizes the important lessons he learned during his two years of simple living. He writes, "Rather than love, than money, than fame, give me truth. I sat at a table where were rich food and wine in abundance, and obsequious attendance, but sincerity and truth were not; and I went away hungry from the inhospitable board." I do love Thoreau, but I have to wonder if he's talking about the kind of truths that feel like a punch to the gut when you hear them. Because notwithstanding that most people say they want to hear the truth, I do think that if given a choice between a hard truth and love, money, and fame, most would choose the latter.

The old cliché is "the truth hurts" and not "the truth is like a warm fuzzy blanket that's nice to snuggle" for a reason. The human brain doesn't enjoy receiving information that threatens our self-esteem, shatters our preexisting beliefs, makes our daily lives more difficult, or threatens our status. Admitting that we're wrong about something, or even partially at fault, isn't easy, even when it's for our own good. When the truth hurts, we want to protect ourselves from the pain, and so we find a way to shut down, stop listening, or otherwise resist. And we're not always aware that it's happening.

FOUR FORMS OF TRUTH RESISTANCE

In the scenario that started this chapter, Pat dodged the truth about his unsuccessful sales call by rationalizing his performance. And while it may seem that Julian's only recourse is to call Pat a bullheaded jerk and write him off as a lost cause who will never admit the truth, there are actually four very different explanations as to why Pat might be resisting the truth. First, let's take a quick look at the four Truth-Killers in Figure 1.1.

Now let's see the four Truth-Killers in action.

First, Pat could have walked out of the meeting saying, "Wow, that CEO was a jerk, but I think I did pretty well considering." In this situation, Pat may be confidently unaware that he made any errors. He may even leave the meeting thinking that he did a great job and would be shocked to hear that Julian thought anything different. This Truth-Killer is called **Confident Unawareness**.

Figure 1.1   Truth-Killers

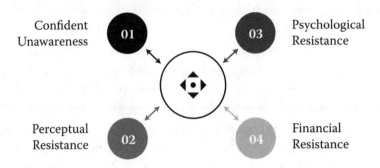

Second, Pat could think the interview went well while also being aware that Julian could have a different opinion. This is akin to Pat saying, "I understand that Julian saw things differently, but that's because Julian wasn't looking at the situation correctly, like I was." Pat won't be receptive to Julian's criticism, but he's also aware that Julian might see things differently. This Truth-Killer is called **Perceptual Resistance**.

Third, Pat could be aware that he messed up. However, in this situation, the pain of admitting his mistake is so threatening to his ego that he rationalizes his mistake by insisting that instead he had actually done something really smart. This Truth-Killer is called **Psychological Resistance**.

Fourth, imagine that Pat receives greater financial reward for lead generation than he does for closing deals. The company has decided to incentivize its salespeople to push open the door, which will allow the law of averages to work to ensure that enough of those leads will become paying customers. In this case, Pat may very well understand that he botched the sales presentation, but because his incentive is to open doors, not close deals, he's not really bothered by the outcome. This Truth-Killer is called **Financial Resistance**.

Based on the study of hundreds of thousands of individuals and leaders, these four Truth-Killers are the biggest reasons why people fail to recognize and accept the truth.

These Truth-Killers run the gamut from the psychological to the economic, and they affect various groups including individuals, families, companies, and countries. Some are seemingly inborn, while others are clearly man-made. And while several weren't discovered until recently, once we know what to look for, they can all be seen throughout human history.

I share the following exploration of each the four Truth-Killers, not to depress you, but rather to show you the very real impediments we face when talking to someone about a tough truth. But if you understand these Truth-Killers, you can anticipate them. And if you anticipate them, you'll find that by having a Truth Talk you can adroitly circumvent the resistance these Truth-Killers create in just about every situation.

Truth-Killer #1: Confident Unawareness

You probably know the Mark Twain quote "It ain't what you don't know that gets you into trouble. It's what you know for sure that just ain't so." It's a great quote that we hear often, and it's a fairly apt description of Confident Unawareness.

Remember the television show *American Idol*? Over the years, *American Idol* did uncover some decent vocalists (I certainly sang along to more than a few Kelly Clarkson songs while driving in the car). But the show generated the greatest notoriety for finding people who were awful during the audition rounds. And it wasn't just that *American Idol* uncovered terrible singers; it's that those same people thought they were amazing. They were shocked that they didn't make it to the finals. This too describes Confident Unawareness.

There are numerous reasons why people might experience Confident Unawareness. Perhaps they were poorly trained. For example, if your lifelong piano teacher told you to keep your hands flat and your shoulders scrunched (two bad techniques), you'd confidently believe that this is the right way to play piano. Or if your running coach from elementary through high school trained you to strike the ground with the heel of your foot rather than the midfoot, you'd be confidently unaware of your flawed technique.

Confident Unawareness also occurs in the workplace. More than 30,000 employees completed a detailed survey about their jobs, and one of the questions was "I know whether my performance is where it should be." Only 29 percent of employees say they "always" know whether their performance is where it should be, with another 14 percent responding "frequently." The remaining 57 percent of employees responded with "never," "rarely," or "occasionally."

We shouldn't be too surprised by the number of employees who are unaware of performance problems. The majority of them simply don't know, and thus haven't been told, whether they're doing a good or bad job. If Pat has a long history of abrupt behavior during sales presentations, for example he frequently shuts down client questions with an ultimatum, and he hasn't yet received any critical feedback on his performance, why wouldn't he believe that he knows what he's doing? Up until Julian called him on his behavior, he's never received any information to the contrary.

Confident Unawareness and the Dunning-Kruger Effect[1]

Sometimes the root of Confident Unawareness isn't poor training or a lack of feedback, but rather a metacognitive inability, or meta-ignorance (ignorance of ignorance). It's called the Dunning-Kruger effect.[2] Coined by Cornell psychologists David Dunning and Justin Kruger, it's a cognitive bias whereby people who are incompetent at something are unable to recognize their own incompetence. And not only do they fail to recognize their own incompetence, but they're also likely to feel confident that they actually are competent.

Consider the quote from Mark Twain that I shared a few paragraphs back. I attributed it to Mark Twain, but how confident are you that Mark Twain really said it? Al Gore (and his team of writers and researchers) were pretty confident when they attributed the quote to Twain in the 2006 documentary film *An Inconvenient Truth*. The words certainly sound like Twain's brand of satirical humor, but it was said by the nineteenth-century American humorist Henry Wheeler Shaw (aka Josh Billings). The actual quote is "It is better to know less than to know so much that ain't so."

Messing up a quote may be a benign example of not knowing what you think you know, but just think of the impact a dangerously bad driver who thinks he is an excellent driver can have, or a machinist who refuses to learn how to safely operate her machine tools because she thinks she already knows it all, or even a manager who lacks any knowledge of how to lead a team but thinks he's an expert leader.

In their landmark study,[3] Dunning and Kruger gave tests to college students on humor, logical reasoning, and grammar. If you've ever wondered why your humor-impaired friends innocently persist in telling jokes that aren't funny, look no further. It's probably the Dunning-Kruger effect. Even though you never laugh and you continually tell them their jokes are lousy, they hold a very different and quite unshakable belief in their ability to tell a great joke.

In the grammar test part of the study, participants took an actual grammar test, and they also rated themselves on how well they felt they did on the test and how well they thought they did compared with their peers. Ideally, if I take a test on a subject I'm clueless about, I should know that I'm clueless and rate myself accordingly. The problem is we sometimes have no idea when we're clueless, and our own cluelessness can lead us to having false confidence. In other words, we rate ourselves with high scores thinking this is the truth.

On the grammar test, like with any college exam, some students scored well and others bombed. For those who bombed, their scores were at the tenth percentile (which means they only scored higher than 10 percent of people). Compared with their peers, their grammar skills were lacking. Yet when they rated how well they thought they did as compared with their peers, those in this tenth percentile group put themselves much higher—somewhere between the sixty-first and sixty-seventh percentile (meaning they thought they scored higher than 61 percent to 67 percent of their peers).

In other words, they lacked the skills to correctly recognize grammar rules, and because they lacked those grammar skills, they also lacked the skills to know that they didn't know grammar. The old cliché "We don't know what we don't know" does a good job of describing the Dunning-Kruger effect.

Dunning-Kruger in the Workplace

Dunning-Kruger isn't limited to college kids. One manager told me that the most challenging work conversations she faces are with employees who have a blind spot when it comes to professional growth. "No matter how many times I point out an opportunity to improve, they just don't see it. They're not receptive to feedback or suggestions, and instead they argue with me or tune me out. And it's almost always the individuals with overt confidence in their abilities."

Professionals typically rate their performance significantly higher than their bosses do. In one meta-analysis involving more than 35,000 people, researchers found minimal correlation (.22) between people's self-rating on performance appraisals and the rating their boss gave them. That means there's not much relationship between the inflated ways we see ourselves and how our boss sees us. This helps explain all the incompetent, low-performing employees who, much to their managers' astonishment, demand better pay, perks, and promotions.

In another David Dunning study, he and his colleagues discovered that MBA students greatly overestimated their emotional intelligence. These folks were around 30 years old and had five to six years of postcollege work experience. When asked to rate how they thought they compared with American adults in general, they placed themselves at the seventy-seventh percentile (they thought they had more emotional intelligence than 77 percent of American adults). But when they took an actual test of emotional intelligence, it turns out they overestimated their scores by about 36 percentile points. Before the test they thought they had higher emotional intelligence than 77 percent of people, but the actual test revealed that they only scored higher than 41 percent of people.

That's a big overestimation. And it gets even worse.

When Dunning's team looked at the worst performers, they found that students whose tests showed them at the tenth percentile (they only scored higher than 10 percent of American adults) had thought that their emotional intelligence was going to be around the seventy-second percentile. They overestimated their emotional intelligence by 62 percentile points!

While the average person overestimates emotional intelligence, the people with the lowest actual emotional intelligence hugely overestimate themselves. In fact, the self-estimates of the lowest performers were almost as high as the highest performers'. When people were shown their actual scores on the emotional intelligence test, guess who were most likely to say that the test wasn't valid or that emotional intelligence wasn't relevant to real life? You guessed it—the people with the lowest scores. And who were least likely to want training or coaching to improve their emotional intelligence? Once again they were the lowest performers.

Identifying people with Confidence Unawareness can be challenging, and when left unchecked, they can create sizable damage. Pam is a project manager at a consulting firm. Six months ago, when she interviewed for the job, she sounded like a winner. Engaged and seemingly sparking with intelligence, Pam had a concrete and detailed response for every behavioral question thrown at her by the organization's best interviewers. She appeared confident, experienced, and ready to hit the ground running. It was a unanimous decision to hire her.

But fast-forward six months, and things look a lot different. If you run into Pam at the coffee machine, she'll tell you that she's a one-woman powerhouse, the glue that holds the company together. But talk to the company's clients and you'll hear strong complaints about how Pam consistently drops the ball. Deadlines are missed, important reports go missing, and calls and e-mails are ignored. The same goes for Pam's direct reports, who regularly vent about what they deem her overwhelming narcissism. Even the vendors are griping. Despite Pam's constant chatter about her full schedule, her superb efficiency, and how downright excellent she is at her job, nothing ever gets done. And as her bosses have learned, constructive feedback goes right over her head. She either twists the feedback into a compliment or confidently redirects the blame onto someone else.

With Dunning-Kruger the mediocre salesperson has no idea about the faster way to close a deal. The subpar doctor doesn't know which new tests could better diagnose an illness. The middling teacher doesn't recognize that there's a new generation of educational tools that improve student comprehension. The pedestrian runner (pun intended) isn't aware of the new training methods that improve performance in less time. In all these cases, if the mediocre salesperson, doctor, teacher, runner, and so on were aware of those advances, they wouldn't be so mediocre.

Most of us have faced the frustration of working or interacting with people who overestimate their abilities without recognizing their inadequacies. Fortunately, there's one area where I'm pretty sure most of us will admit we don't know what we don't know: the writings of Leo Tolstoy. So I'll close this section with a quote: "The most difficult subjects can be explained to the most slow-witted man if he has not formed any idea of them already; but the simplest thing cannot be made clear to the most intelligent man if he is firmly persuaded that he knows already, without a shadow of a doubt, what is laid before him." And yes, Tolstoy really did say that.

Truth-Killer #2: Perceptual Resistance

Most classical music experts agree it's true that Beethoven's Ninth Symphony is an extraordinary work of art, calling it one of the supreme masterpieces of the Western tradition. But when the symphony was completed back in 1824, the reception wasn't quite so unambiguously positive. John Ruskin, considered the leading English art critic of the Victorian era, said, "Beethoven always sounds to me like the upsetting of bags of nails, with here and there an also dropped hammer."[4]

The *Boston Daily Atlas* had this to say: "If the best critics and orchestras have failed to find the meaning of Beethoven's Ninth Symphony, we may well be pardoned if we confess our inability to find any. The Adagio certainly possessed much beauty, but the other movements, particularly the last, appeared to be an incomprehensible union of strange harmonies. Beethoven was deaf when he wrote it."

And a Providence, Rhode Island, newspaper gave this review: "The whole orchestral part of Beethoven's Ninth Symphony I found very wearying indeed. . . . It appeared to be made up of the strange, the ludicrous, the abrupt, the ferocious, and the screechy, with the slightest possible admixture, here and there, of an intelligible melody. . . . The general impression it left on me is that of a concert made up of Indian war whoops and angry wildcats."

I struggle to hear what these critical reviewers heard. Beethoven sounds like "upsetting of bags of nails, with here and there an also dropped hammer"? I've listened to a lot of punk music in my life, so I have some familiarity with music that sounds like spilling nails and dropping hammers. But to my ear, Beethoven's work ranges from lyrical to dramatic, and maybe even forceful. But dropping nails and hammers? No way.

I really don't hear the same symphony as those critical reviewers. And we don't just have differing attitudes about this symphony; we're truly not hearing the same symphony. Their version of the "truth" about the Ninth Symphony is quite different from my version of the "truth." Perhaps the reviewers grew up listening only to music in the simple and light galant style of early Mozart, with its delicacy, clarity, and balance. Maybe Beethoven really was a shock to their worldview. For me, by contrast, after years of listening to the Ramones, Black Flag, and Social Distortion, Beethoven's musical works sound like floating on a cloud of cotton candy while bluebirds sit on my shoulders gently whispering sweet nothings.

With our disparate frames of reference, we "selectively perceive" the Ninth Symphony. We really are hearing different music. And even though the critical reviewers are long dead, if we sat down for coffee to discuss Beethoven, imagine how resistant I'd be to hearing their "truth" (and vice versa).

Selective Perception and Football: A Classic Study

Are you familiar with the Princeton-Dartmouth football game that took place on November 23, 1951? If you are, it's probably not because you're a sports nut; rather it's because this game led to a now-classic study on selective perception.[5]

Psychologists Albert Hastorf at Dartmouth and Hadley Cantril at Princeton describe the setting this way:

It was the last game of the season for both teams and of rather special significance because the Princeton team had won all its games so far and one of its players, Dick Kazmaier, was receiving All-American mention and had just appeared as the cover man on *Time* magazine, and was playing his last game. A few minutes after the opening kick-off, it became apparent that the game was going to be a rough one. The referees were kept busy blowing their whistles and penalizing both sides. In the second quarter, Princeton's star left the game with a broken nose. In the third quarter, a Dartmouth player was taken off the field with a broken leg. Tempers flared both during and after the game.

In the end, Princeton won, but heated discussion about "who was dirtier" continued at both schools for weeks.

The Princeton student newspaper published an article that began:

This observer has never seen quite such a disgusting exhibition of so-called "sport." Both teams were guilty but the blame must be laid primarily on Dartmouth's doorstep. Princeton, obviously the better team, had no reason to rough up Dartmouth. Looking at the situation rationally, we don't see why the Indians should make a deliberate attempt to cripple Dick Kazmaier or any other Princeton player. The Dartmouth psychology, however, is not rational itself.

Meanwhile, an article in the Dartmouth paper read:

The Dartmouth-Princeton game set the stage for the other type of dirty football. A type which may be termed as an unjustifiable accusation. . . . The game was rough and did get a bit out of hand in the third quarter. Yet most of the roughing penalties were called against Princeton while Dartmouth received more of the illegal-use-of-the-hands variety.

If this were just a story about two fan bases that disliked each other and expressed differing opinions about a football game, the story might not be terribly different from what happens after every NFL game in cities around America. But remember, this story turned into a classic psychology study. Albert Hastorf and Hadley Cantril noticed the wildly differing perceptions about the game. And like the eminent scientists they were, they conducted a study. They showed the video of the game to students at each school and had them mark any rules infractions and their severity (mild or flagrant). This is where it gets interesting.

Even though all students saw the same exact game film, Princeton students saw the Dartmouth team make twice as many infractions. And when they rated the severity of those penalties, they saw two "flagrant" to one "mild" on the Dartmouth team, and about one "flagrant" to three "mild" on the Princeton team.

As you can guess, the Dartmouth students saw a very different game. To them, each team made about the same number of infractions. And the severity was about one to one when they judged their own team, and about one "flagrant" to two "mild" when they assessed Princeton's penalties. Princeton saw themselves as victims of Dartmouth's barbarism, while Dartmouth saw the roughness as more equally distributed.

What's most important here is that even though both student bodies watched the same game film, in their minds, they saw very different games. Princeton's "truth" about the game was different from Dartmouth's "truth." The mindsets (psychology, desires, histories, social identities, etc.) that Princeton and Dartmouth students brought to the video viewing differed wildly. And those divergent mental backdrops are what caused them to see the game so differently.

Selective Perception and Customer Service

Perceptual Resistance can, and does, occur everywhere. Inspired by Albert Hastorf and Hadley Cantril, I conducted a modified version of their study using the employees and managers of one of my clients, a hotel chain. Plenty of service organizations, like hotels, casinos, retail, and so on, use secret shoppers or other video surveillance footage to monitor service quality. And while it can be revelatory, it can also reveal significant selective perception problems.

We gathered together the client's secret shopper video footage showing customers checking in to the hotel. Customers approached the front desk, the registration person asked some questions, the customer responded, payment was exchanged for room keys, and the customer left. It's not a terribly complicated process, but there are bound to be some bumps in the road, and that's where you can see big differences in how employees working in registration respond. What if the customer is cranky? Maybe the room isn't ready. Perhaps the customer's credit card is denied? What if the hotel is oversold? The list of potential problems is long.

Working with the hotel executives, I selected five secret shopper videos and we then gathered their 50 managers and supervisors to watch the videos. Following each one, the managers were asked to rate the employee's performance using a five-point scale (with 1 as "poor" service and 5 as "great" service). These ratings would never be used in the employees' performance reviews, and that's partly because the ratings evidenced significant selective perception. On every video, the managers' ratings ranged from 1 to 5, and every number in between.

On the first video, managers watched a late-night check-in. A bleary-eyed customer walked up to the front desk and said, "I've got a reservation under Joe Smith." The hotel employee smiled and said, "Absolutely sir, let me find that. While I'm doing that, how was your trip in? Did you beat the rain? Don't you just love this time of year?" The tired-looking guest grumbled something that sounded like "Uh." The hotel clerk wasn't dissuaded and just kept right on chatting. It went on like this for a few minutes, the clerk's sunny chitchat followed by the guest's grunt, until finally, the transaction was completed and the guest was handed the room key.

When I asked the managers to rate this video, about a dozen rated it great service (5 out of 5) and another dozen said it was poor (1). The remaining managers' ratings were scattered across 2, 3, and 4. How is this possible? Everyone watched the same video, and it was a simple interaction, no credit cards denials, oversold rooms, and so on. When I asked the managers who rated it "great" service to tell me why, I heard feedback including:

- "The clerk was so friendly."
- "The clerk really worked hard to build rapport with the customer."
- "No matter how grouchy the customer was, our employee never let her affect turn negative; she stayed positive and cheerful the entire time."

And when I asked the managers rating it "poor" to tell me why, they said:

- "The clerk didn't read the customer's state of mind; she just strolled through her clichéd customer service script without any modifications."
- "The customer wanted the clerk to be fast and efficient, and instead he got warm, fuzzy, and interminably slow chitchat."
- "I would have gouged my eyes out if I had to listen to that sappy drivel at 11 p.m. when I'm exhausted."

What's clear is that even though these were all managers at the same hotel, with ostensibly the same business goals, they didn't have a common definition of the "truth" about great customer service. Their worldviews, preexisting frames of reference, and so on caused them to selectively perceive this simple customer check-in in wildly divergent ways. And this is just one check-in. Imagine how widespread selective perception is throughout the rest of the organization, and in organizations all around the globe.

I'd love to tell you that selective perception is limited to classical music buffs, college football fans, and hotel managers, but it's not. Have you ever watched a movie with your spouse or a friend and it's as though you weren't even watching the same movie? You loved it and the other person hated it; or vice versa? How many times has this happened in business meetings? Or when evaluating employees' work? Or the CEO's memo?

It's not always easy to tell people the truth when they experience a completely different truth. That's not to say that we can't establish a common understanding, but we shouldn't pretend that it's always automatic.

Truth Killer #3: Psychological Resistance

Jack Nicholson as Colonel Nathan R. Jessup in the military court drama *A Few Good Men* made famous the line "You can't handle the truth." And for good reason, lots of people really can't handle the truth, especially when the truth requires admitting a personal fault, like messing up at work, not acting with concern for others, or not being as talented as we'd like to think we are.

Psychological Resistance occurs when someone holds two psychologically inconsistent beliefs (or attitudes or opinions) that create an unpleasant mental tension called cognitive dissonance. For example, let's say I believe that I'm a charitable and giving person. What happens when I take an action, or hear evidence, that is the obverse of that belief? For example, and this is fictitious, what if my neighbor tells me that I'm the only person in the neighborhood who didn't donate to her food drive for the homeless? I'm going to feel some unpleasant tension. I believe that I'm charitable, and yet I just learned that I acted in an uncharitable way.

This cognitive dissonance hurts my brain, and I'm going to want to do something to reduce this unpleasantness. There are multiple ways I could handle this:

1. I could accept what my neighbor says, admit my mistake, apologize, and start atoning for my failure.
2. I could revise my original belief that I'm charitable (I'll just accept my Scrooge-ness and move on with my life). But a quick look around the planet tells us that admitting fault or discarding decades of positive self-image is not most people's first choice.
3. I could rationalize or self-justify my apparent lack of charitableness by diminishing my neighbor. This could occur as a thought or even a declaration spoken out loud. For example: "I only give to 'legitimate' charities where I know the food will really go to homeless people, and this particular neighbor has always been shifty. Now that I think about it, I'm pretty sure I once saw her pick and eat a grape from the produce section of our local supermarket, and I'm positive she didn't pay for

it. And now I'm going to give to her supposed charity? Oh,
heck no."

4. I could concoct a life philosophy that says "charity begins at
   home" (thus freeing me from any obligation to donate to my
   neighbor's charity). I could even print bumper stickers to that
   effect and proselytize my neighbors.

5. I could tell myself that donating a few cans of food won't make a
   difference, so I'm going to donate when I have more money and
   can truly have an impact.

These are just a few of the potential ways we can respond when
cognitive dissonance invades our brains—all because we don't want
to live in a state of mental conflict. It doesn't feel good to simultaneously hold inconsistent beliefs about ourselves such as "I'm charitable,
but I'm not charitable." It's a maddening existence. So if people learn
some truth that is inconsistent with their existing beliefs about themselves, they are going to somehow change their attitudes or rationalize or diminish this discordant information (even if this information
is the truth).

The stronger or more important people's original belief is, the
more dissonance they will feel. Let's look at another example.

If I consider myself a good cook and yet I cook a terrible meal, the
dissonance I feel will be proportional to the importance of my belief
about being a good cook. But if it's a belief that doesn't matter that
much to me, you can criticize my meal and I'll accept your feedback.
I'll likely suggest we order a pizza instead of eating my lousy food and
not give your criticism another thought. But if you were to say that I
exhibited awful parenting skills when I yelled at my kids, you'd see me
fight that dissonance because being a good father is core to my self-
worth. In a situation like this, I may rationalize my behavior: "The
kids didn't even hear me," or diminish you: "Puh-lease, you wouldn't
know good parenting if it bit you on the rear."

The truth can be hard to hear, especially when it challenges or
violates our self-image or beliefs. The Truth-Killer of Psychological
Resistance occurs when we justify or explain away the discrepancy in
order to alleviate the pain of cognitive dissonance.

The Theory of Cognitive Dissonance

Cognitive dissonance first received scientific recognition in the mid-1950s when social psychologist Leon Festinger and two of his peers gained undercover entry into a small doomsday cult called the Seekers.[6] The group was led by a Chicago homemaker, Dorothy Martin, who claimed the ability to channel superior beings from the planet Clarion.

This alien authority supposedly warned Martin and her followers of a great flood that would destroy the Earth on December 21, 1954. The prophecy stated that only true believers would be spared. This was good news for the Seekers, who were promised safe transport to another planet. Martin channeled clear instructions on how the group should prepare for pickup via flying saucer at midnight on December 17, and the group moved into action, giving up their homes, quitting their jobs, liquidating their savings, and even divorcing nonbelieving spouses.

Festinger's group of researchers didn't actually believe the world would end. They faked their belief so they could join the group and observe the impact of the failed prophecy on the believers' faith. When the world didn't end, would the Seekers reduce the cognitive dissonance by saying, "Whoops, my bad. I guess that was pretty stupid of me," or would they concoct some kind of rationalization?

On the designated night of December 17th, the group gathered in eager anticipation. When a flying saucer failed to appear at midnight, Festinger observed that members of the group appeared nervous. At 12:10 a.m. they looked shocked. By 2 a.m. worry and anxiety prevailed as people sobbed and wept. As I noted earlier, cognitive dissonance can be painful.

Much had been sacrificed both personally and professionally, and some in the group began to openly wonder if the Clarions had abandoned them. As more time elapsed without a saucer in sight, others in the group began to question the validity of the prophecy. Then, at 4:45 a.m., Martin resolved the group's cognitive dissonance when she was gifted with another "prophecy." The message said that the world would be spared because the Seekers "had spread so much light that God had saved the world from destruction."

Festinger had his answer. The cognitive dissonance vanished as the Seekers rationalized that their actions had not been in vain and their prophecy had not been wrong. The formerly media-shy group further reduced their cognitive dissonance by jumping into an urgent media campaign, alerting the press, distributing flyers, and taking to the streets to spread the message that it was only because of their small group's sacrifices and faith that the Earth would still exist on the morning of December 21.

The Seekers may seem like an extreme situation, but cognitive dissonance occurs in all kinds of situations as a way of lessening psychological tension and reducing anxiety when people are faced with feedback or evidence that contradicts an existing belief, attitude, or opinion.

Cognitive Dissonance Happens to Us All

Paradoxically, admitting that we are prone to the irrational mental behavior of cognitive dissonance causes the mental discomfort of cognitive dissonance. Because of this, the awareness that we're experiencing cognitive dissonance tends to elude us. Furthermore, when we witness Psychological Resistance happening in others, even when we've triggered it with our own words, we typically don't realize what is happening. Instead, we make a judgmental leap and don't think twice about it.

Think back to our opening scenario when Julian asks Pat to admit that giving the client an ultimatum resulted in a failed meeting and the loss of a client. Julian probably bruised Pat's ego with this negative feedback, which created some uncomfortable cognitive dissonance in Pat. In order for Pat to relieve himself of the mental pain of these contrary cognitions, he can admit fault, which will involve accepting painful doubts that he's not as good as he likes to believe he is. Or he will have to find a way to deny or rationalize Julian's negative feedback.

Blame and Excuses Are Signs of Psychological Resistance

Diagnosing Psychological Resistance as it occurs in others is possible if we look for the signs. Let's look at some of the blatant signs of Psychological Resistance:

- **Blaming**, or throwing someone else under the bus for our mistakes, is one sign. Blame is the unspoken acknowledgment that constructive feedback is warranted (i.e., the outcomes were subpar) coupled with an unwillingness to admit any personal fault. When verbalized, blame will sound something like this: "Okay, results weren't perfect, but if you want to know where the problem is, go talk to Accounting about why they didn't get the right data to my team before the deadline." Whenever you hear an admission of subpar results followed by someone else's name (or department), you're hearing blame. (Note: This example presumes you're not in, and don't control, Accounting.)
- **Making excuses** is another sign of Psychological Resistance. An excuse is an admission of subpar results plus an admission of fault that is coupled with a host of extenuating factors that no normal human could possibly have overcome. Unlike blame, it won't be another person or department that gets thrown under the bus, but rather your servers, procedures, phone systems, and so on. For example, consider "I didn't get the message," or "The server crashed just as I finished the report," or "We ran out of supplies"—these are all commonly uttered variations of excuses.

Whenever you hear blame or excuses from people, it's likely a sign that they're experiencing psychological pain as they grapple with whatever hard truths you've just told them.

Truth-Killer #4: Financial Resistance

You probably know the Upton Sinclair quote "It is difficult to get a man to understand something, when his salary depends upon his not understanding it!" This aptly describes Jim's situation in facing Financial Resistance.

Jim works in a highly matrixed consulting firm, and he's got to tell teammates, who report to a different boss, that they're not delivering on shared goals. Jim doesn't own his teammates' goals, but he is in a support role to help them implement those goals. So when these teammates fail to hit their goals, it hurts Jim's performance. While Jim gets yelled at for missing goals, his teammates' boss doesn't seem to care too much about whether goals are achieved. Jim has tried lots of different approaches to cajole his teammates into hitting their goals, but they all tell him the same thing: "I'm sorry you're suffering for missing the goals, but we miss goals and nobody minds and we still get paid, so why should we exert all that energy to hit our goals?"

Do you remember the case of *Helicobacter pylori* from the Introduction? *H. pylori* is a bacterium found in the gut that causes peptic ulcers, and Dr. Barry Marshall fought against cognitive dissonance in trying to convince the medical establishment that bacteria can cause ulcers. While he was fighting against something that was already accepted and well known, he was also fighting against another factor: money.

Dr. Marshall began his work in the late 1970s. But earlier in the decade, there was big interest in ulcers, and the acid theory in particular. This theory worked to prove that ulcers were a result of increased acid secretion and/or decreased resistance to acid. The dictum was "no acid, no ulcer."

The National Institutes of Health created a research and treatment center called the Center for Ulcer Research and Education (CURE), which would become a central proponent of the acid theory. Drugs to reduce acid secretion took off: SmithKline launched Tagamet and Glaxo launched Zantac, which the *1986 Guinness Book of World Records* declared was the bestselling drug of all time. Highly popular and profitable drugs like Tagamet and Zantac did help with symptoms of ulcers, but they didn't cure the problem. In fact, some studies found that the relapse rate after cessation of treatment was 50 percent after six months and around 95 percent after one year.

Eventually, Barry Marshall came along and said that patients would be better off replacing expensive drugs with cheap generic antibiotics and bismuth (think Pepto-Bismol). I'm sure you can predict how this theory was received in the medical world. The medical establishment fought him tooth and nail for a decade. The drug companies weren't exactly excited about funding studies that might replace their highly profitable drugs.

Drug companies are run by humans. Doctors are human. And humans in this day and age can be influenced by money. I can sit here and tell you that I would never ever be influenced by such base concerns. But if I had invented the world-record bestselling drug of all time, or if all my research funding came from that drug, I might be somewhat influenced by that fact. I wouldn't *want* to be influenced, and maybe I wouldn't be *consciously aware* of the influence, but the influence would likely still be there.

Financial disincentives are everywhere. If you want a trillion-dollar example, look at the recent financial crisis. Professor Luis Garicano of the London School of Economics, describes it thusly:

> The short term nature of banker's pay—whereby bonuses are accrued over a year—encourages short term, risky decision making. This has to change. Bonuses need to be accrued over longer periods—three or five years. This would mean that if you do something crazy that ends up making you a lot of money this year but, because it is crazy, ends up losing the bank money in five years' time, you will not benefit from it.[7]

Imagine that you're a software developer and your company just instituted a program to reward programmers for the number of bugs they fix. Unless the company also has a metric for tracking who created the bug, the programmers would have a pretty big incentive to produce buggy software so they could turn around and get rewarded for fixing it.

Or imagine that my company just started rewarding people for becoming subject-matter experts. That might increase the company's number of experts, but it might also reduce collaboration. Wouldn't I be incented, even very subtly, to withhold information from my peers so that I would be the subject-matter expert?

Financial disincentives can be subtle or obvious, conscious or unconscious. But they are there, and they do influence our willingness and ability to hear the truth. Fortunately, there are some soldiers for truth out there, including Dr. Leana Wen, an emergency physician and the Baltimore City Health Commissioner. Writing for NPR a few years ago, she said:

> A few doctors, and I'm one of them, are beginning to post information about how we earn our money on a public website and to discuss the financial issues with our patients. We voluntarily disclose potential conflicts and incentives, explain how we are paid, and describe our philosophy of practice regarding other issues, including preventive health, shared decision-making, and end-of-life choices. We believe this can help our patients understand who we are and how this may affect their care.[8]

TRUTH-KILLERS AND TRUTH TALKS

The four Truth-Killers (Confident Unawareness, Perceptual Resistance, Psychological Resistance, and Financial Resistance) provide deeper understanding as to why people avoid, deny, and resist hearing the truth. As you learn how to conduct a Truth Talk, you'll be using these Truth-Killers to assess how much truth your listeners can handle and to help you determine the best approach for delivering the truth.

2

FOCUS ON THE FACTS

Val and Joe are business analysts at ACME Corp who sit in adjoining cubes. Val is just out of college and is looking for the fastest way up the corporate ladder. Joe's been at ACME for a few years. He likes the steady paycheck but finds the work tedious. Joe finds that rocking out to Jimmy Buffett with a small Bluetooth speaker he keeps on his desk helps the day go by faster. One day, after pulling an all-nighter to finish a big report, Val hears Joe jamming to some tunes. Normally he could ignore it, but not today. Val peers over their shared cubicle wall and says, "Hey Joe, your music's at a seven but I could really use it at a four, okay?" Joe looks at Val and then turns his music louder.

Val backs away from the cubicle wall in shock. "What's with this guy?" he wonders to himself. "The other day he rudely shut me down in a meeting, and now he defiantly refuses my request to lower his music! Clearly, he's threatened by anyone with ambition, especially if they're younger than he is. And ironically, he's the child here. I asked him nicely to turn down the music and he throws a tantrum!"

Val is angry, but he also feels fear. Joe and the boss have a good relationship, and Val imagines the boss siding with Joe over this issue. "I'm not going to let that lazy lifer cut into my chance of nabbing the open supervisor position," he thinks. Val decides to take this situation to HR and demand a formal policy change outlawing any music that isn't contained in headphones.

Three feet away, Joe is seething, his mind swirling with some heated thoughts. "I know Val wants that open supervisor position, but if that millennial punk thinks he can prove he's tough enough for the job by ordering me around like a child, he's got another thing coming. Plus, who the heck talks like that? Your music's at a seven? What a dweeb."

While Joe is angry, he is also experiencing fear floating around the edges of his fury. "Jeez," he thinks, "if Val does make supervisor, and he probably will because the boss loves young kiss-ups, he's gonna make my life an absolute nightmare." Joe decides the only course of action is to request a transfer to another department. Resolved, he starts typing an e-mail to the boss.

THE FIRE MODEL

How did the situation with Joe and Val spin out of control so quickly? To diagnose what happened, we need the FIRE Model (Figure 2.1), which explains the four-step process in which we evaluate our surrounding world.

- First, we notice some **Facts**.
- Second, we make **Interpretations** about those facts.
- Third, based on our Interpretations, we experience emotional **Reactions**.
- Fourth, once we experience those emotions, we have some desired **Ends**.

Facts, Interpretations, Reactions, and Ends collectively are the four steps that form the FIRE Model.

The FIRE Model: Facts

Facts are realities that are objectively and independently verifiable. You can videotape and audiotape the facts. The facts are candid, specific, and unemotional, which makes them important players in a

Figure 2.1   FIRE Model

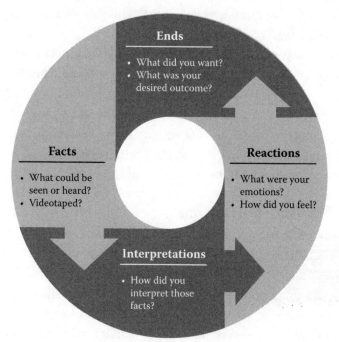

conversation where you want behavioral change to happen. With Joe and Val, the facts are simple: Val uttered 17 words to Joe after which Joe turned up the volume of his music.

The F**I**RE Model: **I**nterpretations

The human brain is a kind of interpretation machine. It doesn't show us the world as it is, but rather as it's useful for us. This is why we all have different perceptions of the world, sometimes radically so. The brain perceives a fact, and then, almost instantaneously, it sifts through all our personal past experiences and knowledge to assign meaning, or intent, to that fact. Sometimes interpretation works in our favor, but other times, not so much.

Imagine you hear a rustling in the bushes outside your bedroom window. You don't unemotionally think, "Hmm, a rustling in the bushes." Depending on your life experience and your history with rustling in the bushes, your brain tries to assign meaning to that fact by making an interpretation. Maybe the interpretation is that the rustling in the bushes is something awful coming to attack you, or maybe you simply think it's likely just the neighbor's stupid dog nosing around again.

There are times when the brain's attempt to connect the dots and assign biased interpretations to the facts can save our lives, like when there is real physical danger. But in most situations, like what transpired between Val and Joe, we don't face life or death; instead we are just dealing with the stresses of everyday living. Unfortunately, unless we mindfully direct it otherwise, the brain doesn't always know the difference between facts and interpretations.

The FIRE Model: Reactions

Once the brain makes the leap from facts to interpretation, and we settle in on a particular interpretation, we have an emotional reaction.

Imagine we're tasked with rating the seriousness of the conflict between Joe and Val. Let's use a seven-point scale, with 1 representing a tiny issue (the kind that could get resolved in a 60-second conversation) and 7 representing a major conflict (where HR, lawyers, and senior executives get involved). If we limit ourselves to the initial facts, those 17 words, we're likely around a 1 or 2. This singular issue should be resolved quickly, especially if Joe and Val can have a quick conversation about the music situation and resolve the obvious misunderstandings. Given what we know about selective perception, Joe and Val might technically have heard the same sentences, but due to their disparate frames of reference, they assigned very different meanings to those words.

But our assessment of the conflict changes when we look at how Val and Joe individually process the facts. Joe's brain takes the facts and interprets that Val is being rude, condescending, and weird while showing off how tough he is to try to gain the supervisor opening. Meanwhile, Val's brain takes the same set of facts and interprets that Joe's noncompliance is due to a hatred of anyone who is young and ambitious.

The conflict between Joe and Val just zoomed from a 1 to a 5. The situation transpired from a simple issue to having HR and the boss involved, requested transfers, and initiation of changes to corporate policies. This is what can happen when the facts get filtered through that infinitely creative, and often misguided, interpretation engine known as the human brain.

You'll also notice that when we talked about the emotions that Joe and Val felt, there were two common feelings—fear and anger, but for very different reasons that were driven by their interpretations, not facts.

It's reasonable that someone might feel irritated by loud music or an insufficiently polite command to turn down said music. But anger? That's a bit intense relative to the offense. And fear seems a bit out of place given that the facts concern a Bluetooth speaker playing some music.

But when we remember that it's typically not the facts that cause intense emotional reactions, it's our interpretations of those facts, emotions like anger and fear make more sense. I too might be afraid and angry if I interpreted the facts to mean someone was going to destroy my career or sabotage my relationship with my boss.

The FIRE Model: Desired Ends

There's one more step in this escalation. Because once we have that emotional reaction, we're then going to have some desired end. We've gone from fact to interpretation to emotional reaction, and now we want something to happen.

If we go back to our reaction to rustling in the bushes and this time interpret the noise as coming from a rare bird, our emotional reaction is excitement, and our desired end might be to grab a camera and document the big moment. But if our interpretation is that a hungry zombie is knocking about in that bush, then our emotional reaction will likely be terror followed by a desired end to either flee or stab it in the brain. In our workplace scenario, Joe's desired end is a transfer, while Val's is that HR rewrite a corporate policy.

Most conversations follow the FIRE Model; we have the facts that lead to interpretations that lead to an emotional reaction that leads to a desired end. As the situation with Joe and Val demonstrates, focusing on interpretation, reactions, and ends can incur plenty of ire, both our own and other people's. And once we slip into the IRE, we lose the possibility of having a fact-based, solutions-focused Truth Talk.

HOW TO USE THE FIRE MODEL BEFORE OPENING YOUR MOUTH

The first rule of any Truth Talk is to stay focused on the facts. The facts are the foundation for your Truth Talk and will ensure that the conversation remains calm, cool, and without any negative emotions. Before opening your mouth to speak, you need to sort through the various thoughts floating around your brain and extricate the facts, separating them from the interpretations, reactions, and ends.

For example, let's say I have an employee named Casey who one morning shows up five minutes late to work. Five minutes late is a fact, but because my brain is an interpretation machine, I immediately want to assign meaning to that fact. Imagine I've had some historic problems with Casey and this influences the way my brain interprets the facts. I assign a negative interpretation to the tardiness, and just like that, I go from "five minutes late" to "Casey is a selfish slacker who doesn't care about the rest of the team and is too lazy to set an alarm clock."

Based on this interpretation, my emotional reaction is I get angry. I get really torqued up, and my desired end is to have this terrible, selfish slacker text me every morning before leaving the house so I know if she will make it to work on time. It may sound a little cartoonish, but this kind of leap into the IRE happens all the time.

In a situation like this, I would likely be so emotionally worked up that chances are slim that I'll sit down with Casey and have a calm, cool, fact-based Truth Talk about the five-minutes of lateness. As my interpretations, reactions, and desired ends (my IRE) consume me, it sets the dynamic for what will likely be a heated and unproductive confrontation.

The other problem with assigning meaning to the facts is that our personal biases may be wrong. While Casey getting to work five minutes late is a fact, in the example above I assume that she is late for negative reasons. But what if instead of pressing the snooze button on her alarm, she was really down in the parking lot talking to my boss about how much she likes working with me and that she thinks I am a great asset to the team. As this example demonstrates, by letting our emotions get the best of us and ignoring the facts, we can wind up making up false stories based on our IRE.

HOW TO PUT THE FIRE MODEL ON PAPER

When preparing for a Truth Talk, a quick and effective approach to separating the Facts from the IRE is to draw four quadrants on a piece of paper and create a FIRE Model diagram, as shown in Figure 2.2. Then simply review your thoughts about the situation and slot each thought into the respective quadrant, as shown in Figure 2.3.

By taking a few minutes to create this simple diagram, I see that in my hypothetical situation with Casey there are 3 words of facts and nearly 50 words of interpretations, reactions, and ends.

This quick exercise really works, and no matter how many times I use this in my real-life Truth Talks, I'm always struck by the power of this visual representation of the FIRE Model. Just a warning: if you skip this step and don't diagram your thoughts and separate the Facts

Figure 2.2   Fire Model diagram

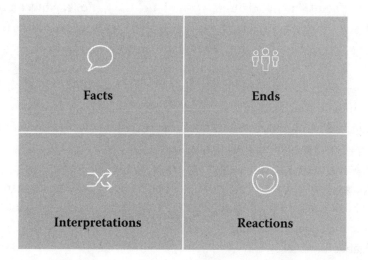

Figure 2.3   Filled-in Fire Model diagram

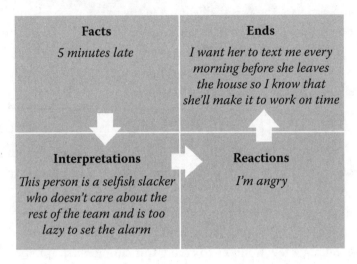

from the IRE, the conversation is vulnerable to all kinds of misinter-pretations, emotional baggage, and ludicrous ends.

HOW TO USE THE FIRE MODEL WHEN YOU RECEIVE TOUGH CRITICISM

One of the additional benefits of employing the FIRE Model is that in the event you receive some hard-to-hear feedback, it will help you dissect it calmly and rationally so you can act toward creating a pro-ductive solution (see Figure 2.4). With the FIRE Model, you can root out any potentially useful feedback while keeping your mind from being overwhelmed by any judgment or negativity you hear.

While the feedback is still fresh in your mind, diagram the FIRE Model and put everything you heard in its appropriate bucket. For example, if your boss gives you some feedback about a mistake you made and he uncorks a bit in doing so, set aside any reactions, inter-pretations, or desired ends you hear.

Now, with just the important issue of the facts to consider, you can determine how to make changes so you don't get that same tough feedback again in the future. The FIRE Model is an exceptional tool for handling feedback and for proving that you can receive and apply valuable feedback.

Figure 2.4   FIRE Model diagram for hard-to-hear feedback

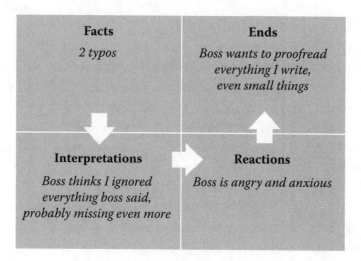

SCOUT FOR THE FACTS

The facts are where you need to focus for a successful Truth Talk. But often, especially in times of stress, we allow our personal biases to cloud the facts. This means we need to stay vigilant as we prepare for, enter, and conduct a Truth Talk.

First, let's review what a fact is. The dictionary definition is "something that truly exists or happens: something that has actual existence. A true piece of information."[1] Add to this what I mentioned earlier about facts being objectively and independently verifiable, where you could video and/or audio record them, and you can start to scout out the facts as opposed to interpretations, reactions, and ends.

But there's a faster, easier, and more accurate way to assess what's fact and what's not: the SCOUT checklist. In general, facts are as follows:

1. **S**pecific
2. **C**andid
3. **O**bjective
4. **U**nemotional
5. **T**imely

Let's dive into how the SCOUT checklist works.

<u>S</u>COUT for the Facts: <u>S</u>pecific

A clear sign that we've left the world of facts and entered the realm of interpretations is the use of words like *always, never, forever, impossible*, and *constantly*. We hear this in statements including "You're always late," "You never get your work done on time," or "You're constantly on the phone." For something to be "always the case" means there is not one single instance where it was otherwise. Arriving on schedule to even one meeting every three years makes the statement "You're always late" false, and so it's not a fact.

Saying that someone is "always late" is not a fact; it's an interpretation, and a negative one at that. But being specific, by referencing the time, date, and location of specific moments, events, situations, actions, and so on, restricts you to only the facts. By keeping your thoughts and words factual, you're keeping yourself relatively calm, which means there's a good chance your words will be heard.

S<u>C</u>OUT for the Facts: <u>C</u>andid

It's not uncommon to feel some anxiety when preparing to have a Truth Talk. But soft-pedaling the seriousness of your feedback will only take you away from the facts. For example, telling an employee, "I checked the records and you missed 10 days of work last month" may incite some conflict. The employee may get upset or try to argue, and that potential for conflict can cause us to feel some anxiety. A common reaction is to soften or obscure the facts with clauses like "but it's not that big a deal" or "I've seen worse" or even "don't worry about it." While soft-pedaling may feel like we're being nice to the recipient and make us feel better about sharing hard truths, it's actually doing more harm than good in the long run.

If the facts are sufficiently important to share, they shouldn't be obscured or diminished. Plus, imagine you're the employee who has missed 10 days of work in the past month and the corporate policy mandates that you'll be terminated after just one more absence within the next 30 days. Would you want soft-pedaling from your boss ("Don't worry, it'll be fine, no biggie") or the candid facts ("One more absence and you're fired")? I'd want the facts because I need that candid truth to have any chance of keeping my job. Telling me not to worry does me a huge disservice and increases the odds that I will get fired.

The irony is that when we soft-pedal the truth, we often tell ourselves that it's for the good of the recipient. But really, if we're honest, we're only doing it to spare ourselves the anticipated discomfort of sharing candid facts.

SCOUT for the Facts: Objective

As I noted earlier, facts are generally verifiable and/or observable, but this doesn't mean that they always must be quantifiable. Some facts are easy to observe but difficult to quantify. One such example is behavior. Suppose you've noticed that your son tends to respond to criticism by blaming others. Let's say he brings home a note from his teacher that says "Jimmy has not handed in any homework for the past two weeks." You question Jimmy about this, and he says, "It wasn't my fault. Sally's always talking to me so I never hear the homework assignment."

It might be difficult to quantify Jimmy's finger-pointing, but it's pretty easy to observe and verify the behavior. Whether at home or at the office, blame typically adheres to a simple grammatical pattern of admitting that there was a failure and then assigning that failure to another person. Setting aside the missing homework for a moment, Jimmy's comment gives you ample evidence to initiate a Truth Talk about eliminating blaming language. It'll be hard for him to say "I'm not blaming anybody!" when you could replay the conversation.

SCOUT for the Facts: Unemotional

Given everything I've said thus far, it's probably clear that facts don't contain emotional language. If someone walks up to your desk and growls, "I'm so mad at you right now," it's a good sign that you're not hearing just facts. But it's not just the obvious emotional outbursts we need to look out for when scouting for the facts; we should also be vigilant for negative emotional labels.

Statements like "Frank's an idiot," "Hunter is clueless," "Pat is overly sensitive," "Sue's entitled," and so on are all negative emotional labels that make it much more difficult for us to calmly and rationally discern the facts. And once we apply these types of labels to a person, we've stopped looking at the facts of a particular situation or behavior, and instead made an interpretation about this person as a whole. This will likely bias how our brain interprets the person's future acts (it's a self-perpetuating spiral away from facts).

Parenthetically, if you want to see an especially vivid example of the influence of emotional language, look at how the press covers the millennial generation. The popular labeling is that millennials are a generation of deluded narcissists with a rocketing sense of entitlement who all feel super special about themselves. Of course, every generation is going to exhibit some behaviors that drive us a little batty (I know that I was a handful growing up). But applying these negative emotional labels makes having a Truth Talk with members of this generation incredibly difficult. How can we be factual and rational when we're entering the conversation with such a negative emotional frame?

SCOUT for the Facts: Timely

Obviously, facts can be millions of years old. If you're reading a history or science book, you're likely exploring facts across decades, centuries, and millennia. And who can forget the immortal words of philosopher George Santayana, "Those who cannot remember the past are condemned to repeat it." I wholeheartedly encourage learning as much history as you can. But when we're discussing the type of facts that typically get shared in Truth Talks (interpersonal or workplace issues), more timely facts lead to more productive and less emotional conversations. History will broaden your mind, but when you're conducting a Truth Talk, limit your conversation to events happening in the here and now.

Dredging up past grievances is bound to make your Truth Talk go haywire. For instance, maybe you're still mad at the way a colleague threw you under the bus in a meeting three years ago. So when you sit down to hash out some new conflict, you casually slip in a comment about how you really can't trust that person given this past action. The disparaging remark made in that meeting three years ago may be a fact. But here's the problem: the further away we get from the actual event, the more our brain replaces the historical facts with interpretations and emotional reactions. You might not remember the exact words said in that meeting, but you clearly remember feeling betrayed by a malicious attack.

It's well established that we tend to remember emotionally charged events better than neutral ones. In a study at Duke University, neuroscientists showed subjects 180 neutral and emotional pictures. One year later, those same people, while being scanned with a functional MRI, had significantly better recollection of the emotional pictures. And not only was there better recall of the emotional pictures, but there was more brain activity in the amygdala and hippocampus.[2] If those brain areas sound familiar, you may recall from biology class that the amygdala is the part of the brain that helps detect threats, as well as helping to process other forms of arousal and emotional stimulation.

Let's look at an example. If you wait three years to tell someone, "You used inappropriate words in a meeting," your frustration has had a lot of time to build. This increases your chances of straying away from the facts and slipping into interpretations, reactions, and ends. Plus, there's not a lot that people can do to remedy a situation that happened in the past, if they even remember it happening!

SELF-DISTANCING: CHANGE YOUR PERSPECTIVE AND KEEP THE FACTS TIMELY

Of course, many of your Truth Talks will be with people with whom you share a rocky past. Maybe your truth partner is a frenemy (a person with whom you're friendly despite a fundamental dislike or rivalry). Or maybe you're still mad about that thing someone did last year, or even 10 years ago, and try as you might to move on and talk about a current issue, this old baggage is hampering your ability to bucket the IRE and focus on the facts. Changing perspective can help.

Typically, when we think about painful experiences from the past, we view the scene from a first-person perspective. We're not a fly on the wall or watching ourselves from a distance—we're immersed and imagining the scene just as we saw it the first time. As the study out of Duke showed us, the problem with that typical approach is that we're reliving the painful moment and experiencing some of the same emotional, and even physical, pain.

However, when we replay conflicts in our head and radically change our visual perspective to only focus on the facts, it has a big impact on our mental state. It's called self-distancing, and it's a scientifically validated phenomenon. Several styles of psychological therapy use variations of self-distancing, from mindfulness-based cognitive therapy to dialectical behavior therapy to neuro-linguistic programming.

Psychologists Özlem Ayduk and Ethan Kross (from UC Berkeley and University of Michigan, respectively) have conducted some powerful research on what happens when we instead replay those negative experiences from a self-distanced, third-person perspective (the video camera in the corner or the fly on the wall).

In one such study, they asked subjects to recall a time when they were enraged by a conflict with a romantic partner or a close friend: preferably a conflict that's unresolved and still highly upsetting. They then analyzed how people did their recalling. Some put themselves right in the moment with a first-person view. But others employed self-distancing; they recalled the conflict as though they were a fly on the wall, almost like an out-of-body experience in which they could see themselves interacting with the romantic partner or friend.[3]

And here's where it gets interesting. People who employed self-distancing—they imagined the situation from the perspective of a fly on the wall—felt much less intense emotional and physical reactions. They felt more closure. And their blood pressure rose less and returned to its normal rate more quickly.

If past baggage is keeping you from the facts, replay the present facts in your mind, but do it from the perspective of the video camera in the corner of the room or the fly on the wall. Don't try to guess what the other person is "really" thinking or feeling. Limit yourself to the spoken words and observable actions. This simple trick of self-distancing can reduce those harmful interpretations, reactions, and ends so you can enter your Truth Talk as your best, most rational self.

PUTTING IT ALL TOGETHER

Once you diagram the FIRE Model to separate the **F**acts from the **IRE**, double-check the facts with the SCOUT checklist to make sure your facts are **S**pecific, **C**andid, **O**bjective, **U**nemotional, and **T**imely. If you hear yourself getting angry, using emotional language, making broad claims with words like *always* and *never,* or talking about something that happened in the past, warning bells should go off in your brain.

Remember, we evaluate our surrounding world through Facts, Interpretations, Reactions, and Ends. Unfortunately, the most important of these (Facts) is the one most often ignored. And the most contentious and volatile (Intentions, Reactions, and Ends) are where we spend most of our time.

We can't have a Truth Talk if we allow our interpretations and emotions to run the show. If we want our truth partners to listen, take accountability, and respond with the desired behavioral changes, we need to stick to the facts. The FIRE Model is a filter that allows you to separate the facts from the IRE to keep tough conversations free from emotional distraction so you don't say something that not only is false but that you may regret.

TAKE THEIR PERSPECTIVE

Forty-one alcoholics walked into a treatment center (I promise, it's not the setup to a bad joke). A few of these study participants were given a self-help book, while the rest were divided among nine therapists to receive different kinds of alcoholism counseling. At the end of a 12-week period, the people who received the self-help book had a 60 percent success rate. The average success rate for the nine counselors was 61 percent.[1]

Now, if we stop there, it seems like good evidence that alcoholism counseling and reading a self-help book deliver the same results. Why would anyone spend money and time on counselors when an inexpensive book works just as well? But the researchers didn't stop there. They looked beyond the average and assessed the results for the individual counselors. A very different conclusion emerged.

When counselors were assessed on a test of perspective-taking and empathy, the three highest scoring had patient success rates (higher levels of treatment engagement and retention in substance abuse programs) of 100 percent, 75 percent, and 100 percent, respectively. The three lowest-scoring counselors had patient success rates of 60 percent, 40 percent, and 25 percent. And this is our big aha moment. Because imagine for a moment that you're one of those 41 patients. You arrive at the treatment center, you fill out some questionnaires to assess your drinking, and then a therapist tells you, "You're currently drinking more than 90 percent of the population."

Yikes.

If you're like most people, hearing a difficult truth like that will trigger some defensiveness. You might say, "That can't be right. Everybody I know drinks that much." If you got one of the therapists that scored low on perspective-taking, he might say back to you, "How can you sit there and tell me that when you filled out the questionnaire yourself? This is how you compare to the rest of the culture. It's right there in front of you." In this situation, the therapist didn't take your perspective at all. His words make you feel even worse, and now your defensiveness is shooting into the stratosphere. You're not motivated to change, and you might even mentally or physically check out of the conversation.

But what if you were assigned to a therapist that scored high on perspective-taking? After you say, "That can't be right. Everybody I know drinks that much," this therapist might respond, "Those results really surprise you. . . . They're not what you expected." This therapist didn't coddle you, but she did take your perspective. You feel understood, and you don't feel judged. And because of this your defensiveness drops. Perhaps you sigh and say, "It's just really hard news to hear. I didn't think my drinking was that bad. I'm really scared about what it's going to take to change." You've taken the first step toward change, encouraged by a therapist who took an approach that acknowledged what it must be like for you to hear the hard truth about your drinking.

WHAT IS PERSPECTIVE-TAKING?

As the above example shows, perspective-taking is a powerful way to get people plugged in and listening when you need to share a hard truth—but what exactly is it? Unlike the technique of self-distancing we learned in Chapter 2, where in order to stay timely with the facts, we assume the objective perspective of the fly on the wall, perspective-taking is seeing the world, or a particular situation, from another person's viewpoint.

Atticus Finch, the moral guide and conscience in Harper Lee's novel *To Kill a Mockingbird*, sets perspective-taking as a key life lesson for his daughter when he tells her, "You never really understand a person until you consider things from his point of view . . . until you climb into his skin and walk around in it." George Herbert Mead, the great American philosopher, called perspective-taking "the capacity to take the role of the other and to adopt alternative perspectives vis-à-vis oneself." And the legendary psychologist Carl Rogers said it's to "perceive the internal frame of reference of another with accuracy, and with the emotional components and meanings which pertain thereto, as if one were the person, but without ever losing the 'as if' condition."

You can call it slipping beneath someone else's skin, walking a mile in his shoes, or something far more complicated, but what perspective-taking definitely is *not* is wallowing around in someone else's feelings. Yes, you perceive the person's personal meanings "as if" they were your own, just as Dr. Rogers said. But you're still you, and you can't engage with the person's emotions. Feeling pity, despair, or any other emotion over someone else's feelings is sympathy. Perspective-taking isn't emotional; instead, it's the cognitive aspect of empathy and the mental process of understanding how someone feels.

Perspective-taking isn't some soft new-age admonition; it gets hard results. In negotiation settings, it leads to greater gains for both parties. For physicians, it's related to higher patient satisfaction, better patient recall of medical information, improved adherence to physician-recommended protocols (such as medication), and more positive health outcomes such as fewer symptoms and improved quality of life. Teachers who use perspective-taking see higher student motivation and effort, which leads to better performance (whether measured by multiple-choice questions or essays). Romantic couples scoring high in perspective-taking report being more satisfied with their relationships, less likely to ruminate over perceived transgressions, and more likely to forgive their partners for these transgressions.

In the realm of Truth Talks, perspective-taking is a critical step to communicating more effectively and in getting other people to understand your message.

PERSPECTIVE-TAKING ISN'T AS EASY AS IT SOUNDS

Taking someone's perspective should be pretty straightforward, right? You just imagine how the person sees the world, and voilà, you've achieved understanding! Sadly, the reality is often much tougher.

Think back to the story of Ignaz Semmelweis, and let's do a little perspective-taking. First, put on Dr. Semmelweis's shoes. Walk down to the morgue and watch your medical students perform a bare-handed autopsy on someone who died yesterday. Then walk up to a patient's room occupied by a new mother dying from a gruesome and painful infection called childbed fever. See your medical student poke and prod this woman with his autopsy-covered hands. Now, have an epiphany and realize that those same hands are causing 1 in 10 new mothers to die.

Seeing the world as Ignaz Semmelweis did, you completely understand why he instantly mandated that all physicians wash their hands with that chlorinated lime solution after performing autopsies. So far, perspective-taking is easy, right? Just like Ignaz Semmelweis, you can probably name a time in your career when you discovered something new that worked really well. Maybe you came up with a new workaround, fixed a software bug, or found a better script for closing deals or handling tough customers. Not only can you picture Dr. Semmelweis's world; you can probably also relate it to your own.

Well, here's where perspective-taking gets tougher. Let's walk in Dr. Semmelweis's shoes for a bit and see how it must have felt to have such a groundbreaking discovery be rejected by everyone around him.

Since your epiphany, you've reduced the death rates of new mothers from 10 in 100 to 1 in a 100. But the other physicians on staff, including the ones to whom you report, think your idea is complete nonsense. In fact, they want you kicked out of Vienna General Hospital. One of your esteemed colleagues writes an article about you saying, "I must judge provisionally that his opinions are not clear enough and his findings not exact enough to qualify as scientifically founded."

Given this, how easy is it to take the perspectives of those other doctors on staff? It's tough, isn't it? Personally, when I'm seeing the world through Dr. Semmelweis's eyes, my first thoughts toward those other doctors are "What's the matter with you. I'm saving lives! Do you want mothers to die? Can't you set your own egos aside for two minutes to see the truth?" In fact, history tells us that those thoughts are similar to the ones Ignaz himself had. And sadly, we know how that turned out (he was beaten to death in a mental hospital).

Mentally seeing Ignaz's perspective is easy, but it's not so easy to see things through the eyes of the physicians who opposed him. Just as we can relate Ignaz's epiphany to our own personal experiences, we can also relate to the frustration he felt when that epiphany was shunned. Haven't you also had a brilliant idea squashed or rejected? Been voted down by people with lesser intellects? Gotten dismissed even though all the facts were on your side?

But regardless of how much we identify with Ignaz Semmelweis, he's not the person whom we need to convince. We don't need to have a Truth Talk with Ignaz; we need to have it with these other doctors. And hard as it may be, if we want the conversation to be a success, if we want those doctors to become truth partners, they're the ones whose perspective we need to take.

USE THE FOUR FORMS OF RESISTANCE AS A FRAMEWORK FOR PERSPECTIVE-TAKING

Here's a little trick to make this exercise easier. Remember our Truth-Killers and the Four Forms of Resistance, from Chapter 1? Let's use them as a framework to understand those other doctors' perspectives in that moment when Dr. Semmelweis barged into the medical staff meeting with his new discovery.

Psychological Resistance

If we're those doctors, is there anything about Dr. Semmelweis's discovery that might create Psychological Resistance or cognitive dissonance? Does his discovery create an unpleasant mental tension that puts us in the position of holding two inconsistent beliefs? Well, if I'm wearing the other doctors' shoes, Semmelweis just said that we doctors, people sworn to "do no harm," are killing new mothers. And he basically said that our time-tested practice of conducting autopsies and then treating patients is deadly. Our beloved mentors, the wisest people we know, taught us this approach. Plus, he wants us to wash our hands with chlorine? Do you know how dangerous that stuff is? And we're supposed to have that poison on our hands while we touch patients? So yes, I'm going to say that we're feeling a lot of Psychological Resistance.

Perceptual Resistance

What about Perceptual Resistance? What Semmelweis sees as a solution to contamination (washing with chlorine and lime juice), we see as bad science. Where was his control group? Or his research proposal? Or detailed peer-reviewed article? He concocts some crazy idea and immediately tests it on his patients? I don't care what his results say; his work was so inconsistent with our accepted research practices that he's probably just seeing a random fluctuation. It's not hard to imagine that we're experiencing some Perceptual Resistance.

Financial Resistance

As for Financial Resistance, we doctors get paid to follow established clinical protocols. Our careers and reputations depend on it. Violating accepted norms of medical practice is a quick sentence to ruin and ostracism. Yup, let's say there's some Financial Resistance here.

Confident Unawareness

And what about Confident Unawareness or the Dunning-Kruger effect; is this a case where people are poorly trained or unable to recognize their own incompetence? It's possible, but here's why I left this one until last. The Dunning-Kruger effect is established science, but it's also akin to an insult. I call it weaponized psychology. Saying that someone is experiencing Dunning-Kruger is very close to calling that person an unaware idiot. It's real, and there are people who fit the Dunning-Kruger description and other forms of Confident Unawareness, but when it comes to taking someone else's perspective, it's a very tricky perspective to take. So for the moment, let's say that the doctors at Vienna General Hospital are sufficiently competent and not falling prey to Confident Unawareness or Dunning-Kruger.

When I run through the four Truth-Killers, one by one, I start to see the Semmelweis story in a slightly different light. Of course Semmelweis was correct. In today's world, even a small child could tell you that it's a bad idea to touch people after dissecting dead bodies. But through this exercise we've gained a bit more understanding about why the doctors at Vienna General Hospital didn't immediately adopt Semmelweis's discovery. Maybe they weren't evil monsters or blithering idiots. Maybe they were normal human beings who rejected Semmelweis's discovery because of their decades of training, personal and professional culture, and clinical incentives.

And maybe, had Dr. Semmelweis taken a slightly different approach to sharing his discovery, had he approached his peers using all the tools in this book including perspective-taking, he would have found a more receptive audience to his groundbreaking truth.

Were there jerks on the medical staff at Vienna General Hospital? Undoubtedly. Were there bad people? Probably. And did Ignaz Semmelweis suffer an unmitigated injustice? Absolutely. I'm in no way victim-blaming. But let's be clear: every one of us has some important truth to share. But whether we're talking to a boss, colleague, employee, customer, spouse, child, or neighbor, if we don't explore that person's perspective as part of our preparation for sharing that truth, the odds are slim that our words will ever get heard.

HOW PERSPECTIVE-TAKING HELPS

It's natural to think of people who disagree with us as opponents or obstacles (or worse, stupid or evil). But the more we adopt that frame, the more the people we most need to share our truths with sense it, and thus the more defensive and resistant they become. One of the quickest ways to make someone defensive and resistant is to begin a conversation by assuming that person is evil or stupid or otherwise flawed. That negativity will ooze out your pores, and people don't listen to someone when they intuit that person thinks poorly of them.

When we take someone else's perspective, we start to see that person in a more positive light. We took the perspective of the doctors at Vienna General, and it helped us see them not as monsters, but as well-trained doctors just doing their job. Now, instead of disdain, we're oozing positivity that sends a message that says, "I come in peace and I have a heartfelt intention to understand you." Which message would you rather hear: "You're an idiot and I'm gonna beat some sense into you," or "I'm not here to fight or attack you; I just want to get on the same page as you." Obviously, the latter message is significantly more appealing.

Psychologically, when we take another's perspective and climb into that person's mind, we kick-start a merger of self and other. My self is "in the person's head," and as I wander around his world, I discover thoughts that feel familiar. I start to see ways that the person is like me, and because I like myself a lot, I start to like him more because it turns out he's more like me than I thought. Even if we don't experience an abiding kinship, perspective-taking decreases any disdain or resentment I might have initially felt. And this, in turn, orients our Truth Talk in a more conversational, and less confrontational, direction.

Let's look at the story of Tina who works for a Palo Alto–based tech company. A few months ago she got a new boss. "When Tim first came onboard, he told me he was excited to hear and implement my ideas," Tina says. "This was great news. I have so many good ideas, and here was my new boss telling me to go ahead and share them. But every time I bring Tim one of my ideas, nothing ever happens. He just nods and says 'great idea' and then forgets everything I said. It's his first job as a manager, and I think he's both incompetent and selfish. I think it's time to start looking for a new job, one where my ideas get heard and utilized."

Tina certainly understands her own perspective, but is she really giving Tim a fair shake? If she took Tim's perspective, she'd learn some things that would likely change her interpretation of the situation. For example, Tim has tried to bring new ideas, his own and Tina's, to his boss, who is the founder and CEO of the company. But he got badly burned. His boss's famous reputation for having a big ego is true, and it's going to be hard to get him to admit to flaws in his company. Tim wants to wait a while and earn his boss's trust and respect before trying again. He's also honestly scared about what would happen if he got a new idea to go through and it failed. It could mean his job. If he's going to put anything in front of the boss, it's gotta be a super and no-fail idea. And so far, no one, including Tina, has come up with that level of innovation.

If Tina slipped into Tim's head and gained his perspective, she'd probably be a lot less angry. She might also redirect her energy from looking for a new job to helping Tim brainstorm, thereby helping him while she helps herself.

Perspective-taking doesn't just create warmer emotions. Looking at this through a coldly pragmatic lens, the more we understand someone else's perspective, the more we learn about how we can best deliver our message so this person remains open to hearing the truth. One study involving pairs of negotiators found that by secretly instructing one side to take the perspective of the other side, the joint gains were greater and the solutions were better. And the side whose perspective was taken was much happier with his or her treatment during the negotiation.

Our Semmelweis exercise, where we used our four Truth-Killers as a framework for understanding the other doctors' perspectives, took just a few minutes of work. This allowed us to already uncover several insights that would help us to present our discovery in a way that would receive a warmer reception. We learned that perhaps the other doctors resisted hearing the truth because we challenged their decades of medical training. If this is the case, we can adapt our Truth Talk to avoid insulting or threatening their previous education. Or perhaps the other doctors were scared by our use of a seemingly dangerous chemical like chlorine, or because our research methods broke with their typical approach. Or maybe they felt our idea would jeopardize their careers. In any of these scenarios, knowing the potential obstacles gives us the insight we need to reframe or rework our message and approach to increase the likelihood that they accept our truth.

We don't live in a world where we can discover an important truth, speak it, and everyone automatically hears it. If we want others to partner in conversation so they can hear the truth, if we want to be master Truth Talkers, we need to understand the perspectives of the people we want and need to embrace, or at least accept, our truth.

Perspective-taking doesn't just make us more effective Truth Talkers. It also significantly improves the receptiveness of our listeners, helping them to become more deeply committed truth partners. First, they'll see that we're trying to take their perspective. And just by virtue of our effort they start to feel more open toward us (who doesn't like someone who's really making an effort on his or her behalf?).

Second, our effort to understand our listeners' perspective enforces that we're not coming to attack or insult. We really, truly want to understand their perspective. And that's a signal that this conversation might just be productive.

Third, if we're successful in taking our truth partner's perspective, we elevate the conversation to a whole new level. When we feel heard and understood, our defensiveness drops; we lower our guard and become more open-minded. So your truth partner is likely to share all sorts of information to help you tailor your message. You may learn about that person's cognitive dissonance, differing perceptions, incentives, and more.

Finally, most people live their lives, consciously or unconsciously, with a "norm of reciprocity." If someone does something for us, we feel a psychological obligation to return the kindness. Or as Cicero put it, "There is no duty more indispensable than that of returning a kindness." When you take your truth partner's perspective, you're subtly and implicitly obligating that person to do the same.

Granted, it would be lovely if everyone took our perspective without our having to make the first move. But that's not how life works. So we make the first move and take others' perspectives, and if we do it correctly, we'll start to see them take ours.

A STUDY OF PERSPECTIVE-TAKING

One of the most important studies on perspective-taking comes from a team of researchers at UCLA. They conducted six different experiments to assess what happens when people feel like someone took their perspective. And, no surprise, every single experiment found that people feel great when someone takes their perspective. Several of the experiments didn't even tell subjects that the other person was successful in taking their perspective (e.g., maybe they tried but failed to put themselves into the person's shoes). But it didn't matter. As long as subjects believed that the other person made the effort to try, they experienced more liking, empathy, and generosity toward the perspective-taker.[2]

But after a few of those experiments, the researchers took it a step further. Subjects were asked to write an essay describing a time a boss had treated them unfairly. Believing that another person was reading their essay (it was really just the researchers), one group of subjects was told that the reader said, "I tried to take his perspective, but I just *couldn't* put myself in his shoes." The other group was told that the reader said, "I tried to take his perspective, and I *could* really put myself in his shoes." When people heard that the reader had successfully taken their perspective, they liked that person 19 percent more. And they felt 78 percent more empathy toward the person.

If you're wondering whether any of this led to tangible benefits, all subjects were told that they would be playing a game with the reader. They were informed that whoever won the game would be entered into a drawing to win money and that the person who went first in the game had the best chance of winning. The researchers then offered the subjects the choice of whether they wanted to go first (and be more likely to win money) or give up their turn to the reader (and be less likely to win money). The subjects who were told that the reader successfully took their perspective were 59 percent more likely to give up their turn (and cost themselves a better chance of winning money)! And all because they believed that the reader took their perspective.

Whether the truth you need to share is focused on trying to improve an employee's performance, stop a colleague from bullying, get a spouse to lose weight, or help a friend to curtail her drinking, the odds that an impassioned speech or a heated argument will create an immediate change in behavior are pretty low. But if you take other people's perspective—if you stand in their shoes and see the world through their eyes—the odds of them hearing and implementing your message skyrocket.

Another important lesson to learn from this study is that you can't force people to take your perspective, especially if you haven't taken theirs first. A Truth Talk won't be effective if you don't first take the other person's perspective. Unfair as that may seem, it's the necessary first step that lowers your truth partner's defensiveness and encourages your partner to reciprocate by taking your perspective in turn.

I'm typically asked, "What if I'm dealing with someone who absolutely refuses to take my perspective in return?" The answer is it doesn't matter. Even unreciprocated perspective-taking delivers tremendous insight into our truth partner's mindset and provides us with crucial information for getting that person to hear and respond to the truth.

THE EMPATHY DEFICIT

Have you found yourself thinking that perspective-taking, and empathy in general, seems to be lacking these days? Not just in one-on-one conversations, but across the whole culture? Well, your intuition is accurate. A recent study of American college students showed that empathy has declined over the last 30 years, and the decline is substantial. Between 1979 and 2009, empathy scores declined between 34 and 48 percent.

I recently conducted a study of more than 30,000 employees and managers. Among the questions I asked was to rate how much "I listen to new ideas even if they seem radically different from my own." This question is a good proxy for perspective-taking; if you're willing to listen to new ideas that are radically different from your own, you're likely to willingly take another's perspective.

The bad news is that only 37 percent of respondents said they always or almost always listened to those new and different ideas. This was a simple, straightforward question with no trickery whatsoever: do you listen to new ideas even if they seem radically different? Yet only 37 percent of people said yes. Meanwhile, 63 percent of folks happily cop to close-mindedness and adopt the mindset of "Nope, I just don't or won't listen to those new ideas."

Parenthetically, Facebook's data scientists recently analyzed to what extent users see articles in their news feed from "ideologically diverse" sources. First, they looked at how many people declared a political affiliation in their user profile (about 9 percent of American Facebook users). Second, they discovered that only about one out of four of people's Facebook friends claim an opposing political ideology. They also found that of the hard news that our Facebook friends share, only 25 percent of the articles we click on cut across ideological lines.[3]

All of this is why it's so important for us to approach our Truth Talks by making the first move in taking the other person's perspective. Especially today, when most people aren't just sitting around feeling empathy and open-mindedness.

PERSONALIZE YOUR TRUTH PARTNER

A trick that makes perspective-taking a whole lot easier is to say the name of the person who will be your truth partner. You can say it in your head or out loud. Then insert the name into the following statement: "I'm going to have a Truth Talk with _____ " (Jane, Bob, etc.). It sounds hokey, I know. But the trick is to individualize that person. When you see Jane or Bob or whomever as a unique individual, it's a lot easier to take people's perspective than when you see them as an anonymous member of a group.

One of the great psychologists of our time, the late Amos Tversky, conducted a study with Donald Redelmeier to see if physicians would recommend different treatments to patients if they thought about these patients as unique individuals rather than as anonymous members of a group of people with the same medical issues.[4]

In the study, physicians were given different medical scenarios and asked to choose the most appropriate treatment. There were two versions of each scenario: one described an individual patient; the other described a group of patients. Here's an example.

The Individual Perspective

H.B. is a young woman well known to her family physician and free from any serious illnesses. She contacts her family physician by phone because of five days of fever without any localizing symptoms. A tentative diagnosis of viral infection is made, symptomatic measures are prescribed, and she is told to stay "in touch." After about 36 hours she phones back reporting feeling about the same: no better, no worse, no new symptoms. The choice must be made between continuing to follow her a little longer by telephone or else telling her to come in now to be examined. Which management would you select for H.B.?

The Group Perspective

Consider young women who are well known to their family physicians and free from any serious illnesses. They might contact their respective family physicians by phone because of five days of fever without any localizing symptoms. Frequently a tentative diagnosis of viral infection is made, symptomatic measures are prescribed, and they are told to stay "in touch." Suppose that after about 36 hours they phone back reporting feeling about the same: no better, no worse, no new symptoms. The choice must be made between continuing to follow them a little longer by telephone or else telling them to come in now to be examined. Which management strategy would you recommend?

The Difference in Perspectives

Notice the difference? In the first scenario, you're thinking about H.B., an individual patient. In the second scenario, you're thinking about a group of patients.

These scenarios were given to doctors in a range of settings where some doctors received the individual scenarios and others received the group scenarios. Now here's the fascinating part: physicians who read the group scenarios recommended just sticking with a phone follow-up anywhere from two to six times as often as those who read the individual scenario. Maybe it's just me, but given what this study shows, I'd rather see my doctor face-to-face.

In another scenario, physicians were asked whether to order an extra blood test to detect a rare but treatable condition for a college student presenting with fatigue, insomnia, and difficulty concentrating. Depending on the kind of physician the researchers asked (university-affiliated, HMO, county hospital, etc.), the doctors who read the individual scenario recommended the extra test (even though it cost more money) anywhere from two to six times as often. Again, I'd like the extra test to rule out the treatable blood condition, wouldn't you?

The Danger of "Grouping"

Once we start thinking about people as being members of a group, we strip away their uniqueness. And once that happens, stereotypes and caricatures emerge. Scroll through your Facebook feed and you'll find generalizing statements like these that fail to account for individuals. For example:

- All guys like this . . .
- Women hate it when you . . .
- Did you know that Muslims believe . . .
- Millennials are so annoying because they . . .
- Old white guys . . .
- Liberals/Conservatives are all . . .
- Well of course he thinks that; he's southern/old/young/etc.

It's common for unique individuals to be reduced to group stereotypes. And while it may be necessary, at times, to talk about groups of people, when you're entering a Truth Talk, it's dangerous. So rather than thinking about having a conversation with employees or executives, or those jerks in the so-and-so department, think about having a conversation with Pat, Chris, Tom, or Sally. The less you see your truth partner as a stereotypical member of a group, the more you'll see the person as a unique and potentially interesting individual.

PERSPECTIVE-TAKING DOESN'T EXCUSE BAD BEHAVIOR

Every so often I hear from managers who ask: "I have an employee who constantly messes up. Why should I take this person's perspective?" For example, take Micah, who says, "Almost every day I have to remind Landry, one of my direct reports, to finish projects, submit invoices, return client calls, and more. Landry makes a big production of apologizing and promises to try harder. But nothing ever changes; I just keep getting the same careless work and drama."

"Have you tried taking Landry's perspective?" I asked.

"I'm not interested in making excuses for bad performance," Micah said. "I just want to get Landry up to speed."

It's a common misconception that taking someone's perspective is the same as excusing bad behavior. It's not. Even when you're dealing with someone who is a consistently poor performer, perspective-taking is simply a way of understanding what's going on inside that person's head so you have the right information to move forward.

When we take Landry's perspective, we learn that this is a job for which she is poorly suited with respect to brains, organizational skills, resilience, and work ethic. Landry doesn't care about tasks and achievement. Landry's happiest years were during high school because of the drama and cliques and soap operas. She wants a social club with lots of friends, not a job.

By tapping into Landry's perspective, Micah can stop the daily performance management kabuki. Micah can now focus on the fact that Landry's a poor fit for the job and doesn't want to undertake the personal transformation necessary to succeed and act accordingly.

In cases like this, perspective-taking reveals when a manager is avoiding taking tough actions. Some employees don't want to change, or even work for you. That's fine; there's a good solution for this situation. But you'll never get to a place of resolution until you stop trying to fix people and start taking their perspective.

4

SET YOUR GOALS

So far we've used the FIRE Model to separate the Facts from the Interpretations, Reactions, and desired Ends (IRE). This helps us to have calm and cool conversations that are free of negative emotions. We've also considered the Truth-Killers that can get in the way of our words being heard. And we've learned how perspective-taking, unemotionally seeing the issues as if through another person's eyes, can help us shape a successful Truth Talk. There's just one more step of preparation before the actual conversation begins, and it's setting a goal for your Truth Talk.

Without a proper goal, it's just too easy to stray from the purpose of a Truth Talk. Sticking to the facts using the FIRE Model prevents us from slipping into the IRE and turning the conversation into an emotional and messy conflict. But steering the conversation in the right direction also requires having a goal.

While goal specifics will vary according to the situation, the essence of a good goal for any Truth Talk is to effect a behavioral change. As the English philosopher Theodore Zeldin said, "Conversation doesn't just reshuffle the cards: it creates new cards."

THREE BAD GOALS TO AVOID

Before we get to what constitutes a good goal for a Truth Talk, I want to highlight three popular goals that are bad goals. Depending on the circumstances, you may feel justified in achieving one or more of these goals. And you may believe that realizing these goals will bring you a sense of real satisfaction. But I promise you, these goals won't bring positive, long-lasting results. The only thing you'll accomplish with these goals is to undermine your Truth Talk.

Bad Goal #1: I Want an Apology

Culturally, we put a high value on apologies. Our life lessons in the importance of saying "I'm sorry" start when we're still young, and we carry into adulthood the expectation of hearing the words "I'm sorry" whenever we're on the receiving end of a transgression. It's understandable why wanting someone to say "I'm sorry" is such a popular goal when there are hard truths at stake. The problem is that apologies usually don't live up to the expectations we have when we think about getting one.

Remember Val and Joe who sit in adjoining cubicles at ACME Corp? Val asked Joe to turn down his music, and in response Joe increased the volume. Let's imagine that Val decides to confront Joe about what just happened and his goal is getting Joe to say he's sorry. Val believes that hearing Joe apologize will remedy the situation and allow them both to move on. Here's how that conversation might go:

> Val: Come on, Joe, are you serious? I asked you nicely to lower the volume. I put up with your music every day, and I never say a word about it. Can't you please, this one time, just say you're sorry and do the right thing?
>
> Joe: Gee, really, every day my music bothers you? I'm sorry I make your life so difficult, but I'm glad you finally got to tell me how you feel. That must take a burden off you. I'm on my way to lunch anyway, so sure, I'll turn the sound down . . . for now.

Well, Val got that apology he was after, sort of. And he succeeded in getting Joe to turn down the volume, sort of. Unfortunately, "sort of" isn't good enough when it comes to tackling most tough truths. It's real, permanent changes that we want. One of the biggest misconceptions about Truth Talks, and difficult conversations in general, is that success equals hearing an apology. A sincere apology is great, if it happens. But as Val learned the hard way, apologies lose all meaning when they are divorced from the way a person really feels.

You can go into a conversation intent on getting an apology, and you might succeed in squeezing one out of someone. And if you hold authority over that person, you might be able to force the words "I'm sorry" through fear or intimidation. And hearing someone say "I'm sorry" may even provide you with a feeling of temporary mollification. But there's no guarantee that what you'll get is a sincere apology that inspires permanent behavioral change.

A Truth Talk is a dialogic process that reduces your truth partner's psychological barriers to hearing, accepting, and acting upon the facts of the hard truths you need to share. Sometimes your truth partner will "see the light" with trumpets, heartfelt apologies, and all the rest. If that happens, great! Enjoy the heck out of it. But don't make getting an apology your goal. Helping your truth partner to *change* is the whole reason you're having this Truth Talk. Browbeating the person until he or she offers an apology will only jeopardize your chances of creating that change.

Bad Goal #2: I Want You to Admit You Were Wrong

Getting people to admit they are wrong is not a way to get them to admit that you are right. Bringing a combative winner-loser mentality of "I want you to admit you were wrong and that I'm right" to a Truth Talk will turn the conversation toxic.

Let's see how it works out for Val when he tries to get Joe to admit he was wrong about turning up the volume on his music.

Val: Come on, Joe, are you serious? I asked you nicely to lower the sound just a little bit and you go and turn it up? Why would you do something like that? What's wrong with you, anyway?

Joe: You know, I don't hear one other person complaining about my music. Besides, I wouldn't have to play my radio in the first

place if you didn't make so much noise. I only do it to drown
you out.

Val: That simply isn't true, Joe, and you know it. Why are you
being so difficult about this? Please, just admit you were wrong
and let's move past this.

Joe: Oh, so first you try to boss me around, and now you're calling me a liar! Most days I can't even hear myself think because
you're so loud. It's no picnic sitting next to you either, you know.

Val may feel justified in wanting Joe to admit he's wrong, but
if you recall our Truth-Killers, you'll remember the myriad mental contortions people can adopt to avoid admitting they're wrong.
Remember, it took the church 300 years to retract its charge of heresy
against Galileo for declaring that the earth revolves around the sun. I
suspect that Joe may take even longer to turn down his tunes, unless
Val changes his approach.

As we've seen, the unpleasant psychological tension people feel
when they mess up can be so intense that they'll hold onto lousy
stocks too long, blame their colleagues, make excuses, and even convince themselves that they saved the earth from destruction by sell-
ing all their personal belongings. And now we want to force them to
admit their mistakes to us and intensely feel that unpleasant psychological tension? Setting a goal to get someone to admit he or she was
wrong is a recipe for an unsuccessful conversation.

Bad Goal #3: I Want You to Feel Bad for What You Did

When there's a hard truth to share with someone, it may seem like
behavioral change is sure to happen if only you can make that person
feel anguish, guilt, or responsibility. No one likes to feel bad, so it
must be a great motivator. Why, you're probably just doing people a
favor when you point out why they should feel bad about something,
right?

Wrong. Setting a goal to get someone to feel bad is never a good
idea. Let's look at how it worked out for Val when he set a goal to
make Joe feel bad for his actions.

Val: Come on, Joe, are you serious? I asked you nicely to lower the sound. How about doing the right thing here?

Joe: Give me a break. My music isn't even that loud. I can barely hear it.

Val: How about a little empathy here, Joe. You know I'm exhausted from pulling an all-nighter. Why are you trying to mess with me?

Joe: First of all, it's not my problem that you had to work late. Second, I'm not the one doing anything wrong. You're the one distracting me from getting my work done. No wonder you get stuck working late all the time. And now, if you'll excuse me, I really need to get back to work.

Val (to himself): That Joe is a creep. I'm going to make him pay for this one way or another . . .

Whether it's being too loud, causing problems with an acidic attitude, being chronically tardy, or manifesting some other undesirable behavior, it may seem plausible that if you get people to feel bad for whatever it is they have done, they'll change, but it doesn't work like that. Even if you believe that making someone feel bad will deliver a valuable life lesson, it's just not a good goal for a Truth Talk.

Do you remember the movie *A Christmas Story*? It's the 1940s adventures of a boy named Ralphie as he tries to convince his parents and Santa to give him a Red Ryder BB gun for Christmas. Along the way, Ralphie makes a few mistakes and gets punished by having his mouth washed out with soap. In anger, Ralphie fantasizes that he goes blind and when his parents ask what happened he says, with dramatic effect, "It . . . It was . . . soap poisoning!"

Ralphie is a movie character, but many of us harbor fantasies in which those who wronged us suffer some karmic retribution. We want them to feel horrible for blinding us with their soap, not completing the error logs, being late to the office, botching the sales presentation, or rejecting our brilliant ideas. But as enjoyable as those fantasies may be, they're ultimately just that: fantasies. A Truth Talk is not the time to exact revenge or enjoy some karmic retribution, and any efforts in that direction will ruin our chances of getting our truth partner to hear, accept, and act on the truth we're sharing.

Now that we know what kinds of goals not to set, let's take a look at how to develop good goals for our Truth Talks.

HOW TO CREATE A GOAL FOR TRUTH TALKS

A Truth Talk isn't about blowing off steam or exacting revenge. The reason you're having this conversation is to create positive change, and this requires a goal that is both rational and strategic. But when we're preparing for a Truth Talk, it's usually in response to an emotionally challenging situation. Our buttons have already been pushed, and that can make rational and strategic feel pretty far out of reach. This is why so many people default to one or more of the bad goals I just described. A technique called 6 Months Later helps take you outside the emotional distraction so you can view your goal objectively. Here's how it works.

The 6 Months Later Technique

Start by picturing yourself and your truth partner interacting six months from now. While envisioning this future interaction, answer these four questions:

1. In six months, what do I want our relationship to be like?
2. In six months, what changes do I want to have occurred?
3. In six months, what do I want to be doing?
4. In six months, what do I want my truth partner to be doing?

The answers to these four questions form your goal. For example, if Val is preparing to have a Truth Talk with Joe about the volume on his music, he might answer these four questions by saying that:

1. In six months our relationship is one of mutual respect where Joe and I can interact without animosity or disagreement.
2. In six months what's changed is that I feel comfortable that if I make a polite request of Joe, he will respond in a calm and positive manner.

3. In six months I want to no longer be having conversations with Joe about petty issues like noise control.
4. In six months I want Joe to understand why it's important for us to work with each other and not against each other. This will be especially important if I get that promotion I'm after.

Val's answers to these four questions tell him that while he wants Joe to change his behavior, he also has a goal to handle this Truth Talk in such a way that the two coworkers end up with greater respect and improved communication. Obviously, storming up to Joe's desk and threatening him to get him to turn down the volume won't help Val achieve his goal. He's going to have to remain rational if he wants to achieve the desired results.

Let's look at another example of the 6 Months Later exercise. I need to have a Truth Talk with my employee Hunter, because he hasn't been filling out the error logs and he responded angrily to my initial request for him to do so. In this case I might answer the four questions by saying that:

1. In six months our relationship is one of mutual respect where I can make requests of Hunter and he responds positively, without anger or sarcasm.
2. In six months what's changed is that I trust Hunter will act on my work requests in a timely manner, and if he is unable to meet a deadline or request, he will express these concerns to me in a calm and factual manner.
3. In six months I want to no longer be having conversations about problems with the error logs.
4. In six months I want Hunter to be completing the error logs as accurately as the department's high performers.

My answers to these four questions tell me that while I want Hunter to change his work performance so that he's completing his error logs like a high performer, I also have a goal to handle this Truth Talk in such a way that Hunter and I end up with greater mutual respect and improved communication. Once again, it's obvious that threatening Hunter to get him to complete the logs won't help me achieve my goal. I'm going to have to remain rational if I want to see the desired results.

It's also clear from this exercise that in order to achieve my goals, I can't just send Hunter an e-mail detailing my instructions. I might get a few error logs completed by doing that, but achieving the other parts of my goal, like increasing our mutual respect and making our communication more comfortable and factual, is going to require a different strategy. I'm going to need some face-to-face time with Hunter, which affords me the communication strengths of tone of voice, two-way interaction, body language, and the opportunity to quickly undo mistakes or understandings.

The Science Behind 6 Months Later

Temporal distancing is the technical name for looking at a situation from a future perspective. And research shows that when we think about a situation from a temporally distant perspective (further in the future), we feel less stressed and negative.

Researchers at UC Berkeley conducted a series of experiments to prove this point. They asked the study subjects to identify the source of stress in their lives that was causing them the most distress at the present moment. Some of them were then asked to reflect on how they might feel about their stressor in the near future (in one week), while others were asked to imagine their feelings in the distant future. Following the reflection, all subjects were asked to rate their feelings, stress, and coping.

The study participants who reflected on the event from the perspective of the distant future were significantly less stressed and negative than those who imagined themselves only one week in the future. The distant future thinkers felt that the current consequences of the problem would fade over time. In response, they felt less worried, fearful, anxious, angry, disappointed, and guilty.[1]

Temporal distancing is a simple mental trick that has tremendous psychological impact. There are a number of ways that the 6 Months Later technique, and temporal distancing in general, reduces our stress and negativity, and by implication, makes us able to focus on setting a positive goal for our Truth Talks.

First, when we think about how things will be in the future, it reminds us that even though we may be irritated or angry right this minute, our feelings aren't permanent. By forcing ourselves to think about the future state of affairs, we're in effect telling our brain, "Hey, look at how much better things are here in the future; all those bad feelings went away."

Second, the future perspective detaches us emotionally from the stress of the current situation. If we ruminate about how irritated we are in this present moment, we're not going to enter this conversation calmly and rationally. So when we take a step out of our current irritation and imagine a world far removed from this one, it offers us greater objectivity.

Third, a wealth of research shows that people tend to view the future with rose-colored glasses. We believe things will be better; we'll have more time, more good days, and less stress. So putting ourselves into the future puts us in a more positive frame of mind and, again, reduces our current negativity and stress.

Once we can see that better future in our mind's eye, any current negative feelings diminish. And when we can push aside those negative feelings, we're far less likely to want to set one of the bad goals listed above. Instead we can focus on setting a goal that is directed at positive change.

GET STRATEGIC WITH YOUR TRUTH TALKS

Once we've used the 6 Months Later technique to create a goal for our Truth Talk, there is one more consideration: strategy. For example, some goals can be handled in a 15-minute conversation, while others may take an hour. And then there will be goals that require several separate conversations. One important planning strategy for your Truth Talk is having, in advance, a clear idea of the temporal needs of the conversation.

Two factors that can help determine strategy, such as whether you're headed into a one-time talk or multiple-conversation process, are (1) the complexity of your goal and (2) the intensity of the resistance you'll face from your truth partner. Let's look at both of these factors in detail.

Strategy Consideration #1: How Complex Is Your Goal?

Answering the four questions in the 6 Months Later technique will help you avoid emotional distraction so you can develop a good goal for your Truth Talk. But the information you provide in answering those questions will also help you to assess whether your goal is a simple goal or a complex goal.

Simple Goals

Simple goals are goals that are more transactional than relational. For instance, maybe there's one behavior that you need someone to correct. Perhaps a coworker stepped on your toes one time, or the boss did something inconsiderate in a singular event.

"I work with someone who, while not my boss, is senior in the department," says Jun. "We usually have a really smooth working relationship, but the other day he overstepped his boundaries and delegated responsibility that falls under my purview. I need to talk to him about what happened to ensure it doesn't happen again. I definitely don't want to be dealing with this situation six months from now."

Jun needs to have a Truth Talk with his coworker to eliminate any chance of repeat behavior. Because there is no history of conflict and the two enjoy what Jun describes as a smooth relationship, a simple goal for a short, one-time conversation that reinforces clear behavioral boundaries will likely provide the solution Jun wants.

The same applies to Jaine, who was recently passed over for a promotion in favor of an external candidate. "Maybe it just wasn't my time," she says, "but I feel pretty confused right now and disappointed. The performance feedback I got from my boss indicated that I was a shoo-in for the promotion. It took me by surprise when I got passed over, especially since our company always promotes from within whenever possible. I want to know what influenced my boss's decision so I can put together a strong development plan. The next time a promotion opportunity presents, I'm going to make sure it goes to me."

Jaine needs to initiate a Truth Talk with her boss, but she isn't particularly worried about the entirety of the relationship or what this situation means for the future. She wants to make sure she's next in line for a promotion, but she doesn't express any anxiety or fear about getting fired.

Both Jun and Jaine are simple, straightforward cases where there's a problematic behavior or fact that needs to be fixed or clarified and the relationship is otherwise fine. Their Truth Talks will only require a simple goal.

Alternatively, and this may sound a little cold, a simple goal could also be a case where you have a relationship that's lower in importance. Perhaps you oversee a department in which the employees only stay for 12 to18 months. You need staff to perform at high levels while they're in your employ, but that's not likely to be a long-term situation. In these types of cases, where you're not particularly worried about the relationship, or it's a just a shorter-term situation, your goal is simple and transactional—you just need to get the work done.

Complex Goals

By contrast, complex goals involve scenarios in which the relationship is more fragile or more important. Sometimes the facts of the situation are serious enough to create a threat.

Such was the case for Andrew, a senior technical underwriter for a global insurance organization. He's been with the company for close to three decades. A few months ago his boss of 20 years, a woman he had great respect for, retired. His new boss, Angela, is 15 years his junior. Andrew isn't opposed to taking direction from a younger boss, but he does take issue with how he sees Angela treating the organization's older-generation employees, especially since he's one of them.

Ever since Angela took charge, Andrew feels like his years of experience, which his former boss called an asset, are meaningless. Angela gives all the prime projects to Andrew's younger coworkers. His job duties have been cut, he's excluded from meetings and decision making for the department, and he was asked to sit out of a recent staff training session. "It's clear I'm not wanted," says Andrew.

Andrew says his "heart and soul" are still with the company and he has several good years in him still to give. When he looks six months into the future, he feels strongly that hunting for a new job isn't in his game plan, nor is filing age discrimination charges. He just wants to be able to bring real value to his work. A Truth Talk is in order, but Andrew is going to need to be delicate in how he approaches Angela. This Truth Talk is going to require a complex goal that may entail having several conversations over a period of time.

Strategy Consideration #2: How Much Resistance Will You Face?

We've already explored the ways people can resist the truth in our discussion of Truth-Killers in Chapter 1. But not all resistance is created equal. Some types of resistance are easier to overcome than others. And the degree of each type of resistance can range from mild and fleeting to severe and hardwired. Let's look at each of the four Truth-Killers and what it means to your Truth Talk.

Truth-Killer #1: Confident Unawareness

Confident Unawareness in its mildest form, especially when it's the result of poor training, technical ignorance, or insufficient feedback, is one of the more easily overcome forms of resistance. When this is the case, all that's often required is a short, one-time conversation and the issue is solved. But the more confident people are in their unawareness, the harder Confident Unawareness is to fix. You are going to encounter people who are so lacking in metacognition that it's difficult to get them retrained, or even to develop the awareness that retraining is required.

"I recently brought in some people from another department to help with a big project," says Jodi. "There was one woman who was completely resistant to following my instructions. Or more to the point, she seemed to believe she knew better than I did what the instructions were. One day I was trying to show her how I wanted a spreadsheet done, and she actually peered at me over her glasses and said, "You do know, dear, that I have an IQ in the triple digits. I can handle this spreadsheet in my sleep." And this was after three days of me telling her she was doing it wrong. If it hadn't been so frustrating because we were on a crazy deadline it would have been funny."

As a rule of thumb, if you've tried three or four times to help someone develop the awareness that improvement is necessary, but that person remains cluelessly confident in his or her awesomeness, you've likely got deep resistance.

Truth-Killer #2: Perceptual Resistance

Let's return to Val and Joe. There's only one set of facts in this situation: Val uttered those 17 words to Joe, and Joe turned up the volume on his speaker. But as we've seen, the two men perceive these facts quite differently. Joe's perception is that Val's request to turn down his music is rude, weird, and condescending and that he's showing his toughness as an audition for the supervisor opening. Val, on the other hand, perceives that Joe's noncompliance to his request to lower the volume is due to a hatred of all persons young and ambitious. If Val wants to have a Truth Talk with Joe, he's clearly up against some Perceptual Resistance.

Perceptual Resistance is frustrating, but it can be overcome. It requires a Truth Talk that builds a common language and aligns the respective facts so both parties can view the world similarly. The temporal needs of a Truth Talk that is challenged by Perceptual Resistance are dependent on the depth of the resistance.

Occasionally, you may find that Perceptual Resistance is occurring alongside other forms of resistance, like Psychological or Financial Resistance. In those cases, what may have originally looked like little resistance becomes something much deeper and you may be looking at more than one conversation.

Truth-Killer #3: Psychological Resistance

In the world of challenging conversations, Psychological Resistance is the form of resistance you'll encounter the most. Whether your conversations are with employees, coworkers, spouses, kids, or whomever, the chances are high that your truth partner will experience at least a twinge of Psychological Resistance. Of course, as you use the techniques in this book, you'll quickly be able to reduce that resistance, but there's likely to be some a priori Psychological Resistance.

What factors increase or decrease Psychological Resistance? In addition to the particulars of your unique situation, power, expectedness, and identity are the three general factors that often influence just how much Psychological Resistance you will or won't experience. Let's look at each factor individually.

Psychological Resistance Influencer #1: Power

Your level of power will usually impact the degree of your truth partner's Psychological Resistance. To demonstrate, let's return to the situation where I want to have a Truth Talk with Hunter, my employee who hasn't been filling out the error logs and who responded angrily to my initial request for him to do so.

Our traditional boss-employee power structure gives me titular power. I possess a job title that conveys "I'm the boss," so it's not only allowable for me to give my direct reports feedback; it's likely a required part of my managerial job role. Hunter may display Psychological Resistance, but because I'm the boss, I probably won't have to make this a very long conversation. There's a story among Amazon veterans that Jeff Bezos once remarked, "Do I need to go down and get the certificate that says I'm CEO of the company to get you to stop challenging me on this?" It's an extreme example, and I'm not saying that it is how Jeff Bezos leads full time, but it clearly demonstrates the advantages titular power can wield.

It's a very different story if I'm Frank and I want to have a conversation with my boss about why he won't return my calls. I'm now without that titular power. It's my boss that has the titular power. And he may believe that not only does his title empower him to be the giver of feedback, but it also shields him from receiving feedback from his direct reports (i.e., me). There are some cultures and companies in which bottom-up feedback (from employee to boss), is a big no-no. And if that's your world, you can expect loads of Psychological Resistance when you ask your boss for a sit-down. This Truth Talk may take several conversations.

You can run into similar dynamics when talking to your coworkers. Picture a hierarchical culture where tough feedback flows from the top to the bottom of the pyramid. In those environments, not only would bottom-up communication be indecorous, but coworker-to-coworker feedback may be similarly misadvised. It's not unusual for the boss to walk into our office and say "We need to talk," but our coworkers? More than a few coworkers will say, "You're not my boss; where do you get off telling me what I need to improve?"

Fortunately, titular power is not the only source of power available. Too many people think, "I lack the authority to have any real power at work," and it becomes an excuse for avoiding tough conversations. It's not only a false belief; it's tough to live in today's world by relying solely on titular power.

The softer and subtler "expert" and "informational" powers are where you want to put your focus. These are the two biggest sources of power, they don't require any formal or titular power, and they are easy to build. Informational and expert powers are how millennials find themselves in charge of companies with billion-dollar market valuations. These members of the younger generation didn't rise to the top because they're so well loved, or because they're wildly connected. Nor did they take a long and winding path through some organizational hierarchy to accumulate titular power. In one success story after another, we see they leveraged their informational and expert power.

Say you bring your boss a new bit of information that will interest her, an article or a study or a proposal with the juicy bits already highlighted. Most bosses don't have the time to read everything out there. You say, "I think you'll find this interesting," and right there you are expanding your pool of political capital, developing informational power with the boss.

Or maybe you invest the time to learn how to use the new software your company is using. This is developing expert power. So the next time the boss has a question about how to run a report, you can step in and say, "I know how to do that. I can run the report for you" or "I'm happy to show you how to do it." Expert power is when you can do things better than other people, and once again, it allows you to expand your power and influence.

In this era where information, not title, is the power source, we can expand our power just by learning, growing, and developing our expertise and informational sources. People will start listening to us because we've exerted the effort to expand our power with them. If you start looking for ways you can help others by sharing your knowledge or expertise to make introductions, improve people's day, and so on, you'll have significantly increased their receptivity to your tough conversations, and that translates to shorter, easier Truth Talks. The caveat is that these power sources are most helpful if we've built them before engaging in challenging conversations. It's awfully contrived to walk into someone's office and say, "Here's some helpful information, and, um, by the way, can I now give you some tough feedback?"

Psychological Resistance Influencer #2: Expectedness

No one likes getting caught off guard, especially when it comes to getting difficult or bad news. So even if the topic of your Truth Talk is perfectly appropriate, and even if you have titular power and it is part of your job to deliver this feedback, expect some surprise and resistance if this is the first time the issue is being discussed.

"My boss called me in to her office the other day and totally unloaded on me," says Juan. "I thought I was in good shape; my professional goals and targets are all getting met, I've got healthy working relationships, and I put in more than adequate overtime. But the boss dug into me about how disappointed she is in my performance and how this is the reason I'm not getting the raise I was expecting. How is it that I never heard a word about my poor performance until now? I've heard someone say the boss is going through a tough divorce. I don't think it's me that's the problem. She's clearly got some personal issues going on, and she's taking it out on me. I'm just going to stay under the radar until things calm down."

If Juan's performance issues had been addressed by his boss in real time as they happened, he likely would have had some idea that this conversation was headed his way. He may not like what he hears any better even if he knows it's coming, but removing the element of surprise will make him a lot less resistant to hearing, accepting, and acting on his boss's feedback.

Some relationships, whether in the workplace, at home, or out in the world, have long histories of tackling tough conversations. Other relationships, by contrast, exist for decades with nary a harsh word ever having been uttered. When you're assessing the resistance you're likely to encounter, always ask yourself whether you've ever had a challenging conversation with this person.

Psychological Resistance Influencer #3: Identity

The final factor that tends to influence Psychological Resistance is the extent to which the issue you're about to discuss poses a threat to your truth partner's identity. For example, I take piano lessons along with my kids. My daughter, who is 12, is already better than me, and my son, who is 9, will be soon. I also started skateboarding with my son, and he was better than me after one month on the ramp. But I'm neither a professional pianist nor a skateboarder, so I can take all sorts of criticism and tough feedback without feeling the slightest bit threatened. Even when I suffered a hernia and a torn posterior cruciate ligament from skateboarding, the pain I felt was physical, not psychological. I enjoy both activities, but my piano or skateboarding competence doesn't represent my identity. By contrast, if I received harsh criticism of my fathering, husbanding, writing, or speaking, I'd feel a great deal more resistance.

I've known CEOs who were self-professed terrible public speakers, and if someone criticized their stage performance, they just smiled and said, "You're right. I'm not a good speaker." But if anyone criticized their strategic thinking, financial acumen, or personnel decisions, fireworks would ensue.

When you're preparing for that tough conversation, try to gauge to what extent the issue you're tackling is central to your truth partner's identify. The more central it is, the more resistance you should expect to get.

Truth-Killer #4: Financial Resistance

Financial Resistance is often the most difficult of the types of resistance. And ironically, this is the type of resistance where your truth partners may explicitly acknowledge awareness of your predicament and wish they could help.

Sally and Tom both work for a financial services firm. Sally is the VP of customer experience, and she is rewarded for generating high customer satisfaction. She doesn't oversee staff, like salespeople or call center reps, so she relies on influence rather than formal authority to accomplish her goals. Tom is the VP of the call center and is under constant pressure to get more calls per hour out of his call center reps. That means shorter calls, faster responses, and, unfortunately for Sally, less emotional connection with customers.

You can see the problem here. Tom is fully aware of Sally's desire for call center reps to spend more time on the phone with each customer as a means to improve customer satisfaction. But her goals seem to fundamentally conflict with his.

Situations like this are often considered "incommensurable"; there's no common standard by which to judge or reach consensus. Sally speaks the language of customer satisfaction, while Tom speaks in terms of calls per hour. One isn't better than the other; they're just using entirely different standards to measure success.

Can incommensurable situations be overcome? Absolutely. But it takes time, a common language and standards, and lots of perspective-taking, and it's probably not going to happen in a single 30-minute conversation. We classify cases like this as deep resistance.

PLOT YOURSELF ON THE GRID AND INTERPRET THE RESULTS

Once you've assessed the complexity of your goals and the depth of the likely resistance you'll receive, you can use the grid in Figure 4.1 to strategize your upcoming Truth Talk. Interpret the results as follows.

Simple Goals and Little Resistance

You're looking at having a straightforward Truth Talk. In this situation, you should be able to quickly get to the heart of the issue, discuss tough issues factually, and achieve a resolution that works for everybody.

Figure 4.1   Goal complexity and resistance grid

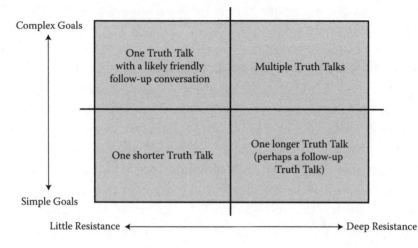

Complex Goals and Little Resistance

When dealing with complex goals, you're in for a slightly longer Truth Talk. Resistance isn't your challenge, but rather the complexity and relational nature of your goals. One approach that works well is to conduct your Truth Talk but also to plan for a follow-up conversation focused on maintaining the relationship. So after the tough stuff, have a lighter chat where all you're doing is solidifying the relationship. Remember, there are relationships that are critical to your success and happiness, and while you need to have the occasional Truth Talk, you also need to infuse those relationships with positive connection.

Simple Goals and Deep Resistance

When simple goals and deep resistance are combined, the results are generally longer and slightly more intense Truth Talks. Your concern here is the resistance, not the relationship, so be prepared, as your message may take a while to get through. If you've been having a Truth Talk for an hour and you don't see much progress being made, think about taking a break and coming back to it again later. People can only take so much intense conversing before they lose steam, focus, and patience. It's why psychologists don't typically schedule three-hour therapy appointments; the emotional exhaustion creates diminishing returns.

Complex Goals and Deep Resistance

You will probably need more than one conversation to accomplish this Truth Talk. Think of it as a multistage Truth Talk. Every situation is a bit different, but a good multistage approach is to focus your first Truth Talk on just creating a picture of the ideal state of affairs.

For example, if Frank, a telecommuter, needs to talk to his boss about how he can't access him when he needs to discuss work, and he suspects the boss will be resistant to hearing this, he might focus his first Truth Talk on defining what great communication looks like when he telecommutes. It's best if this first conversation avoids any exploration of what's going wrong with the current communication. If Frank gets the ball rolling by creating an ideal, just that one conversation could take close to an hour. Then, once Frank and the boss have defined the ideal, they have a platform from which to conduct a second Truth Talk to discuss and fix what isn't working.

The key with all of these scenarios is to think strategically. If you have your facts clear, you've taken the other person's perspective, and you understand the various forms of resistance, you'll have enough information to create an effective strategy for your Truth Talk.

ONE FINAL NOTE: WE CAN'T AVOID TOUGH CONVERSATIONS

In 2013, I published a study that clearly showed that in nearly half of companies, low performers are happier than high performers.[2] This news was shocking because it's not how things are supposed to work. If you're a high performer, you're supposed to be engaged and fulfilled and all the rest. And if you're a low performer, you're supposed to be miserable and disengaged.

But when you're a high performer who's getting stuck doing all the work because the boss won't have a Truth Talk with the low performers, you're likely to be miserable. It doesn't matter if you're Ignaz Semmelweis, Isaac Newton, or a high performer trying your best to do your job; few things in life are more frustrating and demoralizing than carrying the load for someone who doesn't care because the boss just won't deal with that low performer.

That's exactly what my study found. When the *Wall Street Journal* covered the study, many of the reader comments followed the pattern of this one, "Thousands of us are reading this and saying 'sounds like my workplace.'"

It falls on the readers of this book to initiate the necessary tough conversations. It'd be easier, of course, if someone else solved these problems, but that's not likely to happen. And the aforementioned study shows clearly that even on the straightforward topic of dealing with low performers, far too many people are shirking their responsibility for conducting these tough conversations.

5

START A CONVERSATION, NOT A CONFRONTATION

I once knew an executive who was fond of saying, "If I haven't convinced you I'm right, it's because I've been too nice." It was a twist on the popular confrontation technique of "If you don't understand what I'm saying, I'll just say it more forcefully."

Both statements register a level of frustration where, if we're not careful, conversations can become confrontations. People reach their boiling point every day, but confrontations don't make for successful Truth Talks, or much else, for that matter.

After the terrorist attacks of September 11th, depictions of torture on prime-time television increased nearly 700 percent. Americans were scared, angry, and deeply frustrated that we weren't getting the necessary information to prevent further acts of terrorism. Television shows like *24* offered a vicarious catharsis. We saw gunshots to the knee and waterboarding—all resulting in criminals listening to our directives and sharing every morsel of lifesaving intelligence.

After a decade of prime-time torture porn, it's no wonder that so many people buy into the effectiveness of forcibly dominating conversations and bullying people into listening. It seems plausible that talking loudly and forcefully, like Jack Bauer in *24*, will finally get that slacker in accounting to finish running the TPS reports you so desperately need.

I know it can be tempting, and that it looks good on television, but confrontation doesn't work, not even with criminals. Both the U.S. Army and the CIA have released manuals explaining their use of physical and psychological interrogation. The U.S. Army Field Manual states, "Experience indicates that the use of force is not necessary to gain cooperation of sources. Use of force is a poor technique, yields unreliable results, may damage subsequent collection efforts, and can induce the source to say what he thinks the interrogator wants to hear." The CIA's Kubark Counterintelligence Interrogation manual says, "Persons of considerable moral or intellectual stature often find in pain inflicted by others a confirmation of the belief that they are in the hands of inferiors, and their resolve not to submit is strengthened."

If confrontations don't work, what does? Conversations work, especially conversations with open questions, open-mindedness, flexibility, and perspective-taking. One study analyzed more than 600 hours of recorded interrogations of convicted terror suspects.[1] The following is an example from the study that demonstrates the difference between a (nonphysical) confrontation and a conversation.

Imagine that you're a police officer with a suspect named John in custody. First, you tell John about the forensics report you just received: "I have a forensic report here from Dr. Phillips, a forensic scientist expert. I'm going to read you a segment from that statement. Dr. Phillips says, 'The swabs taken from John's hands tested positive for antimony and barium residue consistent with having handled and fired live weapons. Antimony is a common ingredient in gunpowder, and barium is present in the primer used for the firearm.'"

Now, if you wanted to approach this confrontationally, you might say, "Dr. Phillips's report indicates that you have fired a live weapon. That's what really happened, isn't it, John? You have used a firearm, haven't you?" And if you wanted to approach this more conversationally, perhaps you'd say "John, can you think of any reason why your hands might have antimony present?"

The study showed that using the conversational approach when dealing with terrorists decreased their use of counter-interrogation techniques including passive, verbal, and no-comment responding. But it's not just terrorism suspects that don't respond well to confrontations.

In a study of patients in an alcoholic treatment program, researchers found that the more the counselor confronted the patients about their drinking, the more the patients drank (with a very strong .59 correlation). But in situations where counselors did more listening (aka a more conversational approach), patients improved significantly.

I know that criminals and alcoholics may not perfectly represent the people with whom you regularly converse, but these cases do show us a basic truth of human nature—confrontations don't work. Can you remember a time you confronted someone with a difficult truth and afterward that person sincerely said, "Thank you. You've opened my eyes. I accept full responsibility and I'm 100 percent motivated to change!" And then the person actually changed?

And how often has yelling at someone yielded the results you were after? It may have felt good in the moment to emotionally unload, but did you see sustained behavioral change? Confrontation only invites counter-interrogation techniques like refusing to look at interviewers, remaining silent, offering monosyllabic responses, claiming lack of memory, discussing an unrelated topic, providing well-known information, providing a scripted response, retracting previous statements, and giving "no-comment" answers.

I recently conducted a study that looked at the prevalence of workplace behaviors similar to the counter-interrogation techniques. We asked over 3,000 managers to rate four simple questions using a scale ranging from "Always" to "Never":

When people receive tough feedback from me:

1. They offer excuses ("I couldn't get it done because . . .").
2. They shift the blame to others ("It's not my issue because Bob's the one who's responsible . . .").

3. They become aggressive ("I don't know who you think you're criticizing, but I'm the best person here . . .").
4. They shut down and sit there silently and disengage.

For all of those questions, more than 60 percent of managers said that they "Always" or "Almost Always" saw those behaviors. In the workplace we don't call excuses, blame, and aggressiveness "counter-interrogation techniques," but they're basically the same thing. However we choose to label them, they're all behavioral indications that the person we're talking to is not receiving our message.

Let's look at some comments that were shared by people who have suffered the frustration of trying to have a talk about tough truths with someone who just wouldn't listen. Maybe one of these scenarios will resonate with an experience you've recently had:

- "A few weeks ago I spoke to one of my employees about how he isn't achieving the level of strategic thinking required for his job. He nodded his head affirmatively as I spoke, and he promised me he'd try harder, but nothing has changed. I might as well have been talking to the wall."
- "I asked a coworker to handle a document that had a five-day time limit response. But instead, she just returned the document to the adjuster, who was out on vacation, to take care of when he returned. As a result, it took two more employees to obtain the needed documents for a final decision in the remaining three days allowed. When I asked her about it, she just looked at me blankly and said nothing. I have to wonder, did she even hear me when I asked for her help?"
- "I've been working with a developer who is redesigning the company website. Despite my numerous warnings and reports, he continues to design the site according to his own ideas, which for the most part are not SEO-friendly. Most of

my advice is just flat-out ignored. The last straw was when he uploaded the new site to the live server with broken links."

- "Our top client called to inform me that one of our salespeople got rude when discussing the renewal of some of our services. Twice I have scheduled a meeting to talk to my employee about the situation. Both times she called in sick."
- "I really need to talk to one of my people about how he bullies his coworkers in meetings, but every time I try, he shifts the blame to someone else."
- "I have one employee who keeps making the same mistakes over and over. I've corrected him dozens of times, but he never gets it right. I have to think he's just not listening to me."
- "Due to budget cuts we had to cut out some of our employee training. Now whenever I try to give critical feedback, my people come back at me and say it's not their fault because they never got the proper training."

If you're having a conversation about a tough truth with someone, whether it's an employee, colleague, boss, or client, and the person doesn't listen to you, did you really even have a conversation? Sure, words came out of your mouth. But if those words didn't go into the recipient's ears, what's the point?

Blurting out whatever comes to mind mid-rant is confrontation, not conversation. And it should now be clear why confrontation doesn't work. The only surefire way to initiate change is to send a message that awakens a commitment from your truth partner.

THE IDEAS SCRIPT

A five-part process called the IDEAS script lets you send that message to your truth partner. This simple script provides an opening that establishes a dialogue (not a diatribe) and signals to your truth partner that you "come in peace" to learn and share, not fight and yell. Yes, you're going to discuss some tough issues. The IDEAS script doesn't soften the truth. But by following the script, you communicate that you're going to calmly discuss the issues, not shout about them.

The Five Steps of the IDEAS Script

- **Step 1. I:** Invite them to partner
- **Step 2. D:** Disarm yourself
- **Step 3. E:** Eliminate blame
- **Step 4. A:** Affirm their control
- **Step 5. S:** Set a time limit

Each step in the IDEAS script has a distinct purpose. When applied collectively, the steps generate a domino effect that drastically reduces your listener's resistance, making you true partners in conversation. We've seen that verbally punching our way through someone's defenses doesn't work; even the CIA says that confrontation doesn't work. The IDEAS script is effective at getting people to willingly "lower their shields."

Once you practice and get comfortable using this script, all five steps together only take about 30 seconds to deliver. It's a small investment of time with a big payoff. If you skip these steps, you may save yourself 30 seconds, but you will pay for it 100 times over when your truth partner checks out of the conversation by becoming aggressive or turning silent and disengaged.

Let's look at how each step of the IDEAS script works to keep your truth partner feeling safe, open, and receptive to engaging in your Truth Talk.

Step 1. Invite Them to Partner

The first thing to do when starting a Truth Talk is to ask the other person if he or she would be willing to have a conversation with you. This is as simple as asking, "Would you be willing to have a conversation with me about [whatever we need to discuss]?" So, for example, "Would you be willing to have a conversation with me about last week's meeting for the Johnson account?" or "Would you be willing to have a conversation with me about the new financial regulations?"

When you invite someone to partner with you in dialogue, you send the message that the conversation will be a two-way street. You make it clear that while you have an issue you wish to discuss, and that it may be a tough issue, you have no plans to yell, or to extend blame, criticism, or unsolicited advice. The other party feels welcomed in as an equal participant in dialogue, a partner in conversation, where collectively, and nonaggressively, the situation can be discussed and resolved.

Although you have already set a goal for your Truth Talk and know the end result you want, you still need to make the other party feel secure that his or her side will be heard. And this isn't just to be polite. It's quite possible that your truth partner may reveal some additional facts about the situation that will change your desired outcome.

This was the case for Gregory, who was recently asked to head up a new program within his department. "Ever since I took on the new position, one of my teammates, a guy I have to work with every day, has been showing some passive-aggressive behavior," says Gregory. "Things like committing to his part on work and then not seeing it through, talking over me in meetings, and passing me in the hallway without saying hello. I asked him to partner with me in a Truth Talk, and I was really surprised when he shared that he was sore that I had gotten the new position instead of him. I honestly didn't even know that he was interested in it. I still want to stop his bad behavior, but I did change my goal in that I could see ways that I could help him create a professional development plan so next time he gets his chance."

Watch Out for the Word *You*

How someone responds to your invite to partner in a Truth Talk is dependent upon how you ask the question. For instance, you may putatively invite someone to partner in dialogue because you want to yell about something the person has done that offends or bothers you. But you won't get anywhere if your invite says something like, "Will you have a conversation with me about why you've been acting like such an idiot?"

Remember, a Truth Talk isn't for venting or unloading whatever is on your mind; it's about getting the other party to hear your words and to make a change. So whatever the topic is that you want to discuss, keep your description of that topic factual and nonaccusatory.

Saying "Would you be willing to have a conversation with me about why you broke your promise to finish the report on time?" is accusatory. So too is "Would you be willing to have a conversation with me about why you don't return my calls when I'm working from home?"

The word *you* is dangerous when we're starting a Truth Talk for three reasons. First, it's an often loaded, and potentially accusatory, word. Asking someone "Would you like pizza for lunch?" is fine. But when someone comes up to us and says, "You did this" or "You didn't do that," it feels accusatory. It makes us defensive and closed down to productive conversation.

Even when used gently, the word *you* can cause problems. In one study, researchers asked subjects to imagine that they were contacting an online retailer to replace a lost online coupon. The fictional Shopsite.com then responded, requesting some more information. Receiving a message from a supposed customer service rep, some subjects were told, "Once I receive this info, I can investigate the coupon further." Other subjects heard, "Once you send this info, your coupon can be investigated further."

Notice that the only difference between those two responses is the use of the words *I* and *you*. The people who heard the "you" language were 17 percent less satisfied with their customer service and 14 percent less likely to buy from Shopsite.com in the future. And this is an incredibly mild case in which the use of *you* isn't particularly harsh or nasty. But *you* can cause problems even in mild situations.

A second potential problem with the word *you* is that it's often used alongside absolutes, like *always* or *never*. It's not uncommon to hear phrases like "You're always late," "You never hit your deadlines," or "You're just impossible!" Because the word *you* is already potentially inflammatory, it encourages us to keep inflaming our language. And once we're rolling downhill with accusations, it can be hard to stop. It's unreasonable to expect that we can have a free-flowing dialogue with someone when we've just accused that person of being irredeemably bad.

Third, the word *you* is often used in a way that conveys that we've already come to a conclusion. This is a really bad way to start what's supposed to be an open-minded dialogue. Imagine that I asked an employee, "Would you be willing to have a conversation with me about why you didn't get the sales report done on time?" Even though I've asked it as a question, it's pretty clear that I've concluded that the employee didn't get the report done on time. But is that truly a fact? It's likely a fact that I haven't received the sales report, but is that the same thing? Maybe the employee did complete the report, but my e-mail server crashed as it was sent. Or perhaps there was some other good reason (like my boss tasked the person on something else at the last minute). As I mentioned earlier, it's quite possible that your truth partner may reveal some additional facts about the situation that you don't know.

Even if it is a fact that my employee failed to get the report done, my accusatory question is essentially signaling that I want to talk about why that person failed. But the goal of my Truth Talk is to have a conversation about how we can fix things moving forward. So instead I can ask, "Would you be willing to have a conversation with me about the best ways to ensure I get the sales reports by Friday?" This question suggests I'm interested in finding solutions to problems. Yes, we're going to discuss the underlying problems, but it's clear that I'm more interested in finding solutions than I am in discussing all the reasons why my deadline-missing employee is horrible.

So what do we say instead of saying *you*? Try framing the situation more factually and unemotionally. Stay open-minded and remove any judgments about the other person's guilt. Figure 5.1 gives a few examples.

Occasionally someone will say to me, "Jeez, Mark, stop dancing around the issue and just tell this person he's messing up!" I understand the impatience. But if bopping someone in the head with harsh criticism worked, I'd be writing a different kind of book. If you're going to have a Truth Talk, it has to be a real conversation, complete with an open mind, perspective-taking, listening, and facts. Extending a nonjudgmental invitation to partner is the best way to get that conversation started.

Figure 5.1 Framing the situation factually and unemotionally

Bad Way	Better Way
Would you be willing to have a conversation with me about why you don't return my calls when I work from home?	Would you be willing to have a conversation with me about the best way for us to communicate when I'm not in the office?
Would you be willing to have a conversation with me about why you never tell me you're not going to hit a deadline?	Would you be willing to have a conversation with me about how we can make sure deadlines get met?
Would you be willing to have a conversation with me about why you don't complete your error logs?	Would you be willing to have a conversation with me about the error logs?

Step 2: Disarm Yourself

Our next step is to disarm ourselves of judgment in a way that tells our truth partner "I come in peace. I'm not here to yell or blame. I really want to understand and to have a conversation." That's a mouthful, which is why we send this message by saying "I'd like to review the situation and make sure I'm on the same page as you."

If we hope to generate solutions to whatever it is we're discussing, we need to be on the same page with our truth partner. The simple statement "I'd like to review the situation and make sure I'm on the same page as you" communicates the willingness to work toward that end. There are some subtle but powerful twists on the way to word this statement. Notice that I didn't say, "We need to get on the same page." That's because when phrased this way, it sends an aggressive message of "You need to get on my page." If I walk into someone's office and say "We need to get on the same page," that person is going to presume that I'm angry. I might as well have said "We need to get on the same page, Buster!" while giving the "I'm watching you" gesture.

But when I say that I want to "make sure I'm on the same page as you," it puts the onus on me to get us on the same page. Saying you want to make sure you're on the same page doesn't mean that you're necessarily going to agree with the other person, but it does send a reassuring message that you're willing to nonjudgmentally understand a perspective other than your own. This really helps to reduce defensiveness.

I also said, "I'd like to review the situation," which tells my truth partner that I'm not jumping to conclusions, but I really do want to figure out what's going on. Even when I'm pretty sure I already know the details of the situation, it's generally a good idea to review the situation. Because even if it turns out that your initial suspicion was correct, shoving that judgment down someone's throat is virtually guaranteed to make that person resistant.

Christian is a department manager of 25 employees. When he learned that some members of his team were using company time and computers to send e-mails and conduct other personal business, which is strictly against company policy, he called his team into a meeting. His team piled in and Christian launched into attack by saying, "I know you guys know the rules about personal e-mail at work. I'm really disappointed in you all for letting me down. We need to get on the same page on this, and fast. I want this practice to stop, immediately, no exceptions." Not surprisingly, resistance shot up in every direction.

Think of how differently this scenario would have gone if Christian had calmly approached his team and said, "Would you be willing to have a conversation with me about the company's policy on Internet usage? I'd like to review the situation and make sure I'm on the same page as you." He's not being soft, and his goal is still the same; he wants the practice to stop immediately. But because he's approaching the issue calmly and not aggressively, and making the team a partner in the discussion, the members of his team are far more likely to acknowledge that they do know better and agree to stop.

Step 3: Eliminate Blame

A Truth Talk isn't designed to make people feel bad for everything they've done wrong in the past. There's not much point in yelling at someone for messing up or rehashing every past transgression. A Truth Talk should focus on solutions, not on blame. And all you have to say to eliminate blame is "If we find we have different perspectives, we can discuss that and develop a plan for moving forward."

As we've learned, perspective-taking doesn't mean you're necessarily going to share the same perspective as your truth partner. But even if you see things differently, you can still work together to develop a plan that moves in a positive direction. Eliminating blame reassures your truth partner that it's okay if you don't start out on the same page. You can still have a calm and rational conversation to work things out. You're essentially making a contract to stay in a conversational mode, even when you don't agree. Eliminating blame also keeps you away from historical and emotional punishment.

Cady was feeling frustrated because her coworker, Lorrie, often took full credit for their combined work. Cady had tried confronting Lorrie about how she felt, but Lorrie always got defensive quickly and shut down any chance of meaningful conversation. This resulted in a few fights between the two women, and tension between the two is high now.

This time Cady invited Lorrie to partner in a Truth Talk. She told Lorrie up front that she respected her perspective on the situation. "I don't presume that my view is right and yours is wrong," she said. "We may see things differently, and that's okay. But maybe together we can come up with a solution that suits us both." Lorrie wasn't quite ready to admit she'd been wrong, but she was tired of fighting with Cady. When Cady eliminated the blame, that was all it took for Lorrie to drop her guard and enter a solutions-focused conversation.

When you say to your truth partner, "If we find we have different perspectives, we can discuss that and develop a plan for moving forward," you're saying, "We can work this out." It expresses optimism and reassurance and will greatly lower the person's resistance to engaging in the conversation.

Step 4: Affirm Their Control

So far in the IDEAS script we've **invited** the person you are speaking with to partner by asking, "Would you be willing to have a conversation with me about that meeting we had last week?" Next we said,

"I just want to review the situation and make sure I'm on the same page as you, and if we have different perspectives, that's cool. We'll just discuss those and figure out a plan for moving forward." This **disarmed** us of judgment and **eliminated** blame.

The next step is to **affirm** your truth partner's control, and all it takes is asking, "Does that sound okay?"

When you ask, "Does that sound okay?" and your truth partner answers, "Yes, it sounds okay," it emotionally and psychologically flips a switch in his or her brain that says, "I have agreed to this conversation. I come to this conversation as a partner and not like a child who got called down to the principal's office." And this is exactly what you want.

Affirming the person's control strengthens your original invite to partner in dialogue. Your truth partner continues to feel safe that you care about how he or she is doing and what he or she is thinking. It's also a quick litmus test of whether your truth partner remains receptive to your words. If the person replies that it doesn't sound okay, or comes back at you with a rapid-fire list of defensive questions, you can be pretty sure you've lost the person. You'll need to fix this situation before you move on, and I'll show you how to do that in a little while.

Step 5: Set a Time Limit

It's easy to feel defensive when it feels like you're being forced into something without any choice. Your truth partner will naturally feel safer and perform better if, as part of your invitation to partner, you provide some choices as to when the Truth Talk will take place. This can be done by asking, "Do you want to talk now, or would you prefer to wait until after lunch?" You're offering the person a choice, but the catch is that you wrote the options based upon what you need and want.

Offering some choices, even if they are choices limited by your own dictates, provides your truth partner with a sense of control that makes it easier to navigate through a Truth Talk.

PUTTING IT ALL TOGETHER

Here's a quick review of the IDEAS technique and a simple script for each of the five steps:

- **Step 1. I:** Invite them to partner. "Would you be willing to have a conversation with me about XYZ?"
- **Step 2. D:** Disarm yourself. "I'd like to review the situation to make sure I'm on the same page as you."
- **Step 3. E:** Eliminate blame. "And if we have different perspectives, we can discuss those and develop a plan for moving forward."
- **Step 4. A:** Affirm their control. "Does that sound okay to you?"
- **Step 5. S:** Set a time limit. "Do you want to talk now, or would you prefer to wait until after lunch?"

Now let's look at all five steps of the IDEAS script in action. Imagine the following situation: You and a coworker, Bob, cochair a task force. At yesterday's meeting, Bob was supposed to have prepared an updated timeline. However, he showed up empty-handed.

You're angry about this because it made you look unprepared, and your future promotability will be influenced by the success or failure of this task force. So now you're going to have a Truth Talk with Bob to address this problem. Below are two options for starting your conversation.

- **Version A:** "I've got to tell you, Bob, I'm pretty ticked about yesterday. You obviously didn't listen when I said you were in charge of the timeline report. This makes me look like an idiot. If you want to sabotage your career, that's fine, but don't screw up my career too. If you're not going to do something, just tell me so I can do it myself, like everything else."
- **Version B:** "Bob, would you be willing to have a conversation with me about the timeline report? I'd like to review our respective responsibilities to make sure I'm on the same page as you. And if we have a different perspective, which is totally possible, we'll work that out and come up with a plan for the next few weeks. Does that sound okay? Great. Do you have time now, or do you want to wait until after lunch?"

Which version is likely to make Bob receptive to your message? And which version is sending Bob the message that he's under attack and needs to raise his guard? The situation isn't going to change until Bob changes his behavior, and you need his willing participation to make that happen. Hopefully it's clear that Version B is the preferred choice.

Here's the one comeback that some people have to Version B: "But I'm really angry at Bob, and he needs to know that. He let me down and I feel betrayed. Version B makes it sound like I'm letting his behavior slide, and I can't allow that."

That's a very legitimate response. We've all felt those same thoughts, and we've all had that same emotional itch cry out to be scratched. But here's the problem: We need Bob to fix his behavior and improve his performance. And the question is whether making Bob defensive is the best way to accomplish that.

Version A is virtually guaranteed to make Bob defensive. And if his defensiveness makes him aggressive, you're going to have a fight on your hands. Remember, you can't beat him into submission, and if Bob becomes passive, he'll endure your emotional browbeating, but he may subtly sabotage you down the road.

Keep in mind that this is only the preamble to our core message. In the subsequent chapters, I'll show you how to deliver the tough message to Bob that he did, in fact, fail to meet his obligation. But for now, it's sufficient to get him to lower his resistance and accept your invitation to have a real dialogue.

THE POWER OF QUESTIONS

A theme throughout this book is the power of asking questions, sometimes even numerous times. The IDEAS script is a great example of this. Notice how there's a pretty even split between asking questions and making statements? That's by design. The purpose of the IDEAS script is to turn a potential confrontation into a conversation, to move from shouting accusations back and forth to dialoguing with each other. And the only way we're going to make that transformation is by drawing the other person out with questions.

As a rough heuristic, Truth Talks try to achieve a roughly 50-50 split between questions and statements. You won't always be able to make this work perfectly, but it's a good number to keep in the back of your mind. If you find that your Truth Talk consists mostly of you making speeches, you're no longer having a conversation. If you keep reminding yourself, "I want a roughly even split between questions and statements," you'll catch yourself more quickly when you start making long speeches.

WHAT IF YOU INVITE THEM TO PARTNER AND THEY SAY NO?

When you ask questions, like in the IDEAS script, there's always the risk that the other person will say, "No! I don't want to have a conversation with you." It's a lot less common an occurrence than we imagine, but it does happen on occasion. Don't be afraid of hearing no. It's actually okay.

When people say no, they're telling us that they're worried about where the conversation is headed. Maybe they've made some judgments about us, or they're terrified of tough conversations, or they're afraid of being blamed or attacked. We can respond to those fears by saying, "I don't care. You're going to listen to what I have to say!" But hopefully you understand the futility of that approach. Not only will it increase any existing feelings of fear or resistance; it also prevents us from ever learning the specific nature of their unwillingness to engage in this conversation.

Instead, when someone tells us no, we're going to respond with the question, "May I ask why?" This usually does the trick. It's an uncomfortable question to answer and may even prompt a response of "I was just kidding. I'll talk." But the goal in asking "May I ask why?" is to discover the source of the resistance, and when we respond with thoughtfulness and curiosity, we're further demonstrating our commitment to understanding the person's perspective.

Remember how earlier we learned that perspective-taking doesn't just make us more effective Truth Talkers; it also significantly improves the receptiveness of the other person. When truth partners see that we're trying to take their perspective, they start to feel more receptive to our perspective. The same concept applies here. When people lash out and say, "No, I won't talk with you," they're expecting us to react poorly. So when we react thoughtfully and with curiosity, we're flipping the script and demonstrating that this is truly a different kind of conversation.

Talking to her new boss about his micromanaging wasn't a conversation Joy was looking forward to. But she knew her value as a high performer and was feeling disengaged by the constant request for progress updates. So she took a deep breath, walked into her boss's office, and spoke the opening line of a Truth Talk, "Would you be willing to have a conversation with me about how I'm meeting my work deadlines?"

"It's not a good time," was her boss's reply.

Joy immediately responded with another question. "May I ask why?" she said, and her boss gave her a pained look.

Joy didn't let it go. "I just want to see if I'm on the same page as you. We may have very different perspectives here, and that's okay. I'm hoping we can work together to find a solution. Does that sound okay to you?"

"Look, Joy. I know what you're driving at, and I'm sorry you feel I'm micromanaging you."

"If you can't talk right now, what about after lunch or even first thing tomorrow morning?" asked Joy.

"Okay, let's just do this now," was her boss's reply. "What you don't know, and I'm not trying to redirect the blame here, is the level of stress I'm under from my boss. I need to be able to answer to him at any time where all my employees are on their projects, and I have 25 people on my team. The only way I can manage is to micromanage."

"I have an idea for how you can get the continued updates that you need while giving me the autonomy I want," Joy said. "Would you be interested in hearing it?"

"Absolutely," her boss replied, gesturing for Joy to take a seat. "Let me hear what you've got."

Ironically, some of the best Truth Talks you'll have will be ones where your truth partner starts out as deeply resistant. But because of your commitment to open conversation, he or she will turn into an incredibly thoughtful and open conversation partner.

WHAT IF YOU MESS UP?

Truth Talks get easier each time you have one, but we will all make mistakes. The most important thing is to learn from the experience. One day you will find yourself in the midst of a Truth Talk that's going along just great, and then, kaboom: you put your foot over the line, or more likely in your mouth. And without any warning, out comes a rush of blame, criticism, attacks, unsolicited advice, and more, and your Truth Talk takes a nosedive.

It's okay. Remember, you're only human. And at least you're trying to make a difference. You're taking an active part to create a world where people can talk to each other without defensiveness, anger, turf wars, and all the other nonsense that wastes so much time. So when you mess up, take a deep breath, and do whatever it takes to get yourself a do-over.

When your truth partner becomes highly defensive and resistant to your Truth Talk, and nothing that you've tried thus far makes him or her budge, it's time to abort the current conversation. This means a big step backward, taken without hesitation or reservation. It also means delivering a sincere apology and asking if you can please try again.

Let's move out of the workplace and into the home front for a moment and see what it's like to mess up and try again. Imagine you're having a friendly chat with your spouse about where to go for dinner that night. Perhaps the neighbors down the street took you out a few weeks ago, and it's your turn to reciprocate. All is calm, but then, out of nowhere, your spouse's eyes cloud over, his mouth tightens, and you can almost see the tiny hairs on his arms stand on end.

Your spouse bursts out with the following statement, "Do you have any idea how stressed I am about work? I have absolutely no time for myself anymore. And now *you* want me to make time to go out to dinner with some people I don't even like. Sometimes I don't know why I even bother coming home."

You feel the slap of blame the *you* word delivers, and your anger and resistance kick into high gear. While you build your defenses, you silently (and sometimes not so silently) plot and think, "I have a challenging job too. I'm also hungry; I have a new dress, and I'm definitely going out to dinner with the neighbors tonight, with or without you." And so sets the scene for a battle.

But then your spouse's body language relaxes and he smiles, and right there in front of you is the person you fell in love with saying, "I'm really sorry, honey. I know I just attacked you with some really dumb words. I'm tired, and I spoke without thinking. I'm happy to have dinner with the neighbors tonight. Just give me an hour to relax." After your spouse gets through with his apology, he gives you a big hug. You know in your heart he's really sincere and you forgive him. You probably even abandon the idea of dining out and offer to pick up the lo mein if he calls in the order.

WHAT'S FORGIVABLE AND WHAT'S NOT

When you feel a conversation is escalating out of control, there is a way to take it back and get your listener to grant you a do-over. And most times all it takes is saying a sincere "I'm sorry." The key is in being truly sincere. There are some things for which you can apologize, and some things you can't. And if you apologize for the wrong thing, you can kiss your do-over goodbye.

Mistakes of competence such as slipping back into blame mode or giving unsolicited advice are typically forgivable. Everybody messes up at some point in life, and it's always easier to forgive a mistake if it's one you've already made, or one you can see yourself making in the future. So if you know what's good for you, eat some humble pie and admit you sounded like a jerk. If you can do it, and do it sincerely, your Truth Talk will likely be back on track before you have to take another bite.

What is not forgivable is a lapse of integrity. Our apology will accomplish nothing, or even make things worse, if we say, "I'm really sorry I acted like a jerk. You really hurt me, and I wanted to hurt you back." All that does is cast the blame on the other party. And forget about trying to get away with, "I'm sorry you're angry." All that really says is, "I really don't care that you're angry. You did something bad to me, and you deserve to suffer."

A true apology has to be a real admission of wrongdoing, one that doesn't turn the blame over to the other party. It doesn't matter what made you lose your cool. That's not what you're apologizing for. All you can truly and sincerely apologize for are your own actions and competences in carrying out those actions that caused you to lose your cool.

WHAT IF YOU'RE THE ONE WHO GETS ATTACKED?

We've discussed why brute force is counterproductive to a tough conversation. But what if, despite your best efforts, you still find yourself under attack? Is it still possible to stop someone from attacking you and bring that person into a deep conversation or Truth Talk? The answer is yes, but not until you call off your attacker and get the person to a place of calm and reason.

For many of us, our initial instinct when we find ourselves under attack is to strike out and, quite possibly, take down our attacker. But that's not going to help you to achieve your objective. When under attack, it's time to call in some heavy hitters to win the battle. And the first four factors of IDEAS are really going to help:

- **I:** Invite them to partner
- **D:** Disarm yourself
- **E:** Eliminate blame
- **A:** Affirm their control

And then you need to throw a twist on the IDEA—it starts with THE.

THE IDEA

THE IDEA is your best option for turning your attacker into a willing conversation partner. We've already explored how IDEA works, so let's take a look at its predecessor, THE:

- **T:** Take a Second
- **H:** Halt
- **E:** Empathize

THE: Take a Second

What do most people do when they are verbally attacked? Often they tell their attacker to back off and to take a breather. But if you tell your attacker to chill out, you are blaming him or her for the bad situation. And as a bonus, you threw in some free and unasked-for advice on how the person needs to go about fixing the problem. The best approach to take with an attacker is to say, "Wow, I think I need a second here." Calmly and quietly let it be known that you need to take a step back and process.

You want to get your attacker to retreat, but it has to be done nonthreateningly. When you say, "Wow, I think I need a second," it doesn't imply you're angry or defensive, only that you need a little time. However, it does send the subtle message that things have gone a little over the top.

Saying "Whoa" or "Wow" lets your attacker know that his or her behavior is inappropriate without an actual admission that you think the person is being bad. This will catch your attacker's attention in a much bigger way than will blatantly saying, "Hey, you're being a jerk."

THE: Halt

It may be you need more than a second, and from the look of things, so does your attacker. But once again, you have no business telling anybody what to do; you can only speak for yourself and your own needs.

There are many good reasons to postpone a Truth Talk including hunger, anger, loneliness, and exhaustion. Be sensitive to all your emotions, and don't hesitate to call a time-out if you think it will help the situation.

THE: Empathize

Empathy isn't always easy to express, but when it really counts, you need to make sure you sound sincere. At its core, empathy is the acknowledgment and validation of another person's feelings. And it can be expressed simply by saying, "You sound really angry (or upset, frustrated, and so on)."

Empathy is not a prelude to psychoanalysis. There's no need to explore why your attacker wasn't hugged enough as a child. But empathy is an opening to de-escalate some of the attacker's intense emotions so the person can more effectively partner in dialogue and help resolve whatever issues are at hand.

Imagine your teenage son storms into the house after school and says, "I hate this stinking neighborhood." An unempathic response might sound something like, "Do you know how much we had to pay to buy a house in this neighborhood? And we did it just so you could go to a decent school. How about a little gratitude?" On the other hand, an empathic statement might sound something like, "Sounds like you're pretty ticked" or "Jeez, sounds like something pretty bad must have happened."

When you've got an attacker blocking your way to speaking the truth, a little heartfelt empathy can go a long way. Don't get defensive when you're hit with someone's strong emotions; that will only exacerbate the attacker's feelings. Let your attacker know that you hear he or she is angry, or upset, or whatever, and that you care. Most of the time that's all it takes to dissolve the person's negative emotions.

There's no place in a Truth Talk for confrontation and the defensiveness it invites. Instead, break down the Walls of Defensiveness by initiating a conversation with IDEAS: Invite them to partner, Disarm yourself, Eliminate blame, Affirm their control, and Set a time limit. If your invitation is refused, ask why. And if you slip up and say the wrong thing, apologize and start again.

Or if you're the one being attacked, take on your attacker in a nonconfrontational way by asking for a time-out or even postponing the conversation, and always choose empathy over defensiveness.

I'm not promising that you'll never come up against the walls of defensiveness if you follow the scripts and suggestions in this chapter.

People, and life, are just too unpredictable to make that promise. But by using the tools and techniques in this chapter, you will be able to take down those walls and open the opportunity for a Truth Talk.

6

CREATE A WORD PICTURE

You've probably heard this story, but it bears retelling.

Once upon a time, there were six blind men living in a village, someplace where elephants roamed freely. Being blind, these guys had no idea what an elephant looked like, so the villagers told them, "Hey, go over there and you can touch the elephant." They wandered over, and the first blind guy touched the elephant's leg and said, "Dude, this thing is a pillar." (He probably didn't say "dude," but you get the idea.) The second fellow touched the tail and said, "You're nuts; it's a rope." The third man put his hands on the tusk and declared, "You guys are crazy; it's a tree branch." The fourth guy groped the elephant's ear and exclaimed, "It's a big floppy fan." The fifth dude, touching the elephant's belly, shook his head and said, "It's a huge wall." Finally, the sixth blind man touched the trunk and said, "You're all wrong; it's like a pipe." Then, due to their differing perspectives, the six men got into a big fight and argued for hours about which of them was right.

Typically, the morals of this story are that it's hard to see the whole truth with our limited and self-focused perspectives and we should work harder to understand each other's perspectives. And those are good morals. But there's another moral that often gets short shrift:

when everyone has a different definition of the truth, an argument is virtually guaranteed.

Quadrafale manages the blackjack dealers at a large Las Vegas casino. It's time for annual performance reviews, and she's starting with Frond. Frond's performance is good but not great. His technical skills are very good, but his customer service wavers from very good when his table is full to seriously lacking effort, typically when his table is empty. Quadrafale calls Frond into her office and says, "Frond, I'm giving you a 'Meets Expectations' on this year's review. Your technical skills are excellent, but your customer service could use some improvement."

Frond looks at her in disbelief; "What are you talking about with 'Meets Expectations'? I'm one of the best dealers in the entire casino!"

"That's not how I see it, Frond," Quadrafale responds. "I think your customer service could use some improvement. Specifically, I'd like to see you be more courteous to the guests. And really show them that they're your top priority."

"What does that even mean?" asks Frond.

"You know, be more courteous. It's not a complicated concept," replies Quadrafale.

Frond sarcastically retorts, "So I should let them win every hand? I mean that would show them how much I value them, right?"

Quadrafale feels her blood pressure rise as she says, "Frond, if you can't understand a concept this simple, I should change your rating to 'Fails to Meet Expectations.'"

This boss-employee conversation has taken place in practically every company on earth. It's not always about customer service, of course, but about any topic where a manager wants an employee to improve. Instead of six blind men debating what constitutes an elephant, it's two people debating the meaning of customer service (or accuracy, communication, responsiveness, attention to detail, etc.). But the end result is still the same, with confusion, disagreement, and, ultimately, bad feelings on both sides. The tragedy here is that despite its ubiquity, this painful conversation could easily be prevented. If we start conversations by defining instead of debating, we can avoid this type of confusion and disagreement.

The lack of a clear definition dooms everything from performance reviews to marital disputes to scientific studies. Back in 2011, British researchers published a study showing that exercise and cognitive-behavioral therapy could help people with chronic fatigue syndrome.[1] It was a startling finding because this is a disease with subjective symptoms, no known cause, and, thus, no known cure. But it turns out that there was a problem with the study—you guessed it, the very definition of chronic fatigue syndrome.

The researchers took study participants suffering from disabling and unexplained fatigue lasting at least six months. The problem is that those symptoms could include people with depression, an illness that can be treated with exercise and cognitive-behavioral therapy. By contrast, better studies will exclude subjects whose only symptom is fatigue and require that subjects have other neurological or physiological symptoms. As the many critics pointed out, the lack of a clear definition of chronic fatigue syndrome doomed the British study.

What percentage of employees have carpal tunnel syndrome? Once again, it all depends on how you define the illness. One study found that the incidence could be as low as 2.5 percent and as high as 11 percent of employees, depending on whether carpal tunnel syndrome was defined by reported symptoms, a physical exam, a nerve test, or all three. One has to wonder how many painful arguments occurred between patients and doctors simply because the criteria for a diagnosis of chronic fatigue or carpal tunnel syndrome were not clearly defined or agreed upon.

One of my studies asked more than 30,000 employees to rate the statement "I know whether my performance is where it should be." In an ideal world, every person in every job would say, "I always know!" But that's not what the study found. Only 29 percent of people said they "Always" know whether their performance is where it should be. By contrast, 36 percent of folks said they "Never" or "Rarely" know and 21 percent said they only "Occasionally" know. It's no wonder managers and employees have disagreements about whether their performance meets or exceeds expectations; more than half of employees don't have a clear idea about whether they're doing a good job.

Whether it's debates about elephants, disagreements over what constitutes customer service, employees not knowing if they're doing a good job, or an unclear definition of a disease, far too many disagreements occur because we don't have a clear and shared definition.

HOW DO YOU CREATE A SHARED DEFINITION?

Let's return to Quadrafale and Frond. But this time, let's imagine that before they started their conversation, the two of them sat down and together established a clear definition of "customer service."

First they identify what constitutes bad customer service. They decide that bad customer service is when an employee tells customers no or "We can't do that." Bad customer service, they also agree, is when we don't acknowledge customers who walk up to our blackjack table, or we acknowledge them with only one or two words (e.g., "hey" or "whassup"). And they also decide that bad customer service is not empathizing with an angry customer. For example, saying something dismissive like "them's the breaks" to a customer who just lost money at our table.

Prepared with this definition of bad customer service, Quadrafale and Frond then sketch a definition of good customer service. They decide that instead of telling customers no, good customer service involves saying, "Of course we can do that" or "I'm not sure, but I can definitely find out for you." It's also greeting customers with a smile and complete sentences or questions. For example, "How are you enjoying your stay here?" or "My name is Frond. It's great to meet you." And good customer service, they agree, involves empathizing with angry customers. For example, saying, "I'm so sorry you experienced that."

Finally, Quadrafale and Frond create a definition of great customer service, making it a step beyond "good" customer service. For example, after telling a customer, "I'm not sure, but I can definitely find out for you," great customer service involves knowing all the other departments in the casino so the solution can be found within

10 minutes. Great service is not just greeting customers with complete sentences, but also engaging them in conversations, such as inviting them to sit at our blackjack table.

If Quadrafale and Frond had been equipped with this clear definition of bad, good, and great customer service, the performance review wouldn't have resulted in a fight. And it would not in any way have resembled the miserable chastising that typifies most performance reviews.

Not only would this robust definition of customer service have prevented a fight, but Quadrafale would also have been able to make this a true conversation. Now she can say to Frond, "Using these definitions, and based on your work over the past six months, which of the categories, bad, good, and great, do you think best describes your customer service?" Beginning a tough conversation like this, with a question rather than some judgmental statement, positions Quadrafale and Frond to engage in calm, rational, fact-based, and two-way dialogue in which Frond will take ownership of his performance.

In the next chapter we'll explore the conversational techniques for getting your conversation partner to take ownership. In this chapter, I'm going to show you how to create the clear and shared definitions that make that ownership possible.

WHAT IS A WORD PICTURE?

Quadrafale and Frond created what I call a Word Picture. A Word Picture is a tripartite definition that transforms abstract concepts into concrete examples that anyone can understand. There's a lot in that definition, so let's unpack it piece by piece.

Word Pictures Have Three Parts

Quadrafale and Frond's definition of customer service did more than just describe good customer service; their definition also portrayed great and bad customer service. It's critical that there not be any confusion about whether Frond's customer service was bad, good, or great. Confusion leads to arguments and bitterness, and that's precisely what Quadrafale wants to avoid.

By using this tripartite definition (bad, good, and great) and providing concrete examples of each, Quadrafale is borrowing from an instructional approach called Concept Attainment. In a nutshell, Concept Attainment involves learning an abstract concept through studying examples and nonexamples.

Do you remember the Sesame Street song "One of These Things Is Not Like the Others"? Well, that uses some advanced cognitive psychology—Concept Attainment. For example, to teach about the characteristics of a square, Grover or Big Bird has you look at a bunch of squares (examples), but there's one triangle (the nonexample) hanging out in the middle of all those squares. Or you learn about the characteristics of an apple by looking at apples (examples) and then an orange or a banana or a pear (nonexamples). By analyzing those examples and nonexamples, you very quickly figure out the characteristics that define apples (or squares, or whatever).

The research shows that we learn the characteristics of apples faster and more thoroughly with these examples and nonexamples than we do if we listen to a lecture on the characteristics of apples and then go out into the world and try to apply that abstract knowledge to specific situations. In one of the many studies on this topic, students who were only taught a theoretical concept averaged a 76 percent on their tests. But when students received just three examples and nonexamples of that concept, their scores jumped to 88 percent.[2]

In the world of tough conversations, it's a good idea to create examples and nonexamples, but I also recommend creating super-examples. These are the great examples. With Quadrafale and Frond, bad customer service represents the nonexamples, good service the examples, and great service the super-examples. People understand abstract concepts faster and better with examples: when they're taught how to do something well, how not to do something, and how to do that something incredibly well.

Elaine is the CEO of a consulting firm. Her executive team is filled with brilliant minds, but collectively they have a problem: they're passive-aggressive. On the surface, their weekly meetings seem collaborative, agreeable, and harmonious. But when the executives leave the room, they go back to their respective departments and talk trash about their colleagues. For example, the head of sales leaves a meeting and says to his team, "The CFO is such a shortsighted tight-wad that we can't price our services competitively." Or the CFO tells the finance team, "If those idiots could actually sell our value, they wouldn't need to discount all the time." And on it goes.

Two weeks ago, Elaine let loose on her executives. "We've got a passive-aggressive culture, and it needs to stop," she said. "From now on, we're going to disclose our issues in this room, and nothing gets carried outside of here." Her executives vigorously nodded in agreement. And, of course, once they left the room, they went back to their respective departments and told their teams, "Wow, Elaine really let loose on the other executives because they all speak out of school."

The company grapevine immediately told Elaine that her scolding had failed. So rather than repeat an unsuccessful strategy, at their next meeting, Elaine tells her team, "Folks, today we're building a Word Picture to define 'executive communication.' And we're going to start by defining nonexamples of open communication. I'll kick things off: we're doing a bad job of communicating if we tell any of our employees even one word that was said in this meeting."

A shocked CFO interrupts by saying, "But what are we supposed to tell our team when they ask what we discussed?"

"That's a great question," says Elaine, "and the answer will help us define good communication. Anyone care to offer a suggestion?"

The CIO says, "How about we all just say, 'It was a private meeting, so I'm going to abide by that.'" And then the head of marketing chimes in, "If we want to really kick it up a notch and take our communication from good to great, we could each gather our employees and say, 'I've been too quick and loose with my comments about other executives, and I'm stopping that behavior.'"

The discussion continues for an hour, and when they are done, they have three lists: examples of bad, good, and great communication. Or put another way, they have nonexamples, examples, and super-examples. Through these examples, every executive gains a crystal clear understanding of what he or she can and cannot say outside that room. This shared understanding of bad, good, and great communication is key to creating an executive team environment where tough issues can be discussed openly and without passive-aggressive resentment.

Word Pictures Use Concrete Language

Great Word Pictures, and effective communication in general, depend on the use of concrete rather than abstract language.

Many organizations have standards or codes of conduct for their employees. And typically those codes of conduct contain supposed guidelines for having open, honest, and direct communication. I analyzed the communication guidelines from more than 100 organizations and found that lots of companies are giving the same advice to their employees and leaders. For example, versions of the following phrases were used by more than two-thirds of the organizations I analyzed:

- "Disagree without being disagreeable."
- "Focus on the issue, not the individual."
- "Be honest, fair, and open in your communication."
- "Treat one another respectfully."
- "Be professional in your communications."

While the sentiments expressed in all of these statements are lovely, the language used is abstract and thus open to interpretation. For example, I could create a clear picture in my head of what it means to be disagreeable, but the chances are high that what I would picture is different from what you would picture. Some people think that being disagreeable requires ad hominem attacks or a loud voice, while others think disagreeableness means not wearing a smile. The obvious problem is that if we don't share the same picture of disagreeableness, we will struggle mightily to "disagree without being disagreeable."

Providing examples, nonexamples, and super-examples will go a long way toward improving this confusion. But so too will using more concrete and less abstract language. Simply put, concrete language evokes sensory imagery in your mind, while abstract language does not.

For example, "happy clown," "spittle-flecked lips," and "white-knuckled" are very concrete phrases. Upon reading these words, your mind immediately conjures images. By contrast, phrases like "useful purpose," "original finding," and "reasonable request" lack concreteness; they're considered abstract words.

Here's why this matters; concrete words, phrases, and sentences have consistently been found to be more comprehensible, memorable, and interesting than abstract language.[3] And when you're trying to deliver a tough message or resolve a disagreement, you want your truth partner to comprehend and remember your message.

The prevailing theory for why concrete language is so much more comprehensible, memorable, and interesting is that we cognitively have two separate but interconnected systems, one for verbal representations and one for nonverbal (imagery) representations. Abstract language only gets to access the verbal side, but concrete language, because you can "picture" the words, gets to access both the verbal and nonverbal systems. In its most simplistic form, you can think of this "dual coding theory" as a neuropsychological version of "two is better than one."

We know that the phrase "treat one another respectfully" is a popular admonition; it's also pretty abstract. If we want to define "respect" more concretely, maybe we could say something like "treat one another respectfully" means:

- We speak factually and avoid negative emotion words like *angry, hate, sucks, stupid, moron,* etc.
- We don't talk about people if they're not present.
- We take turns when engaging in one-on-one conversation, with a 50-50 split in speaking time.
- When speaking with groups of three or more people, we ask each person to contribute to the conversation.
- Before we start a conversation, we ask the person whether he or she is willing to have a conversation with us.

Now, I'm not saying this is the ultimate definition of what it means to treat one another respectfully; you can define respectfully however you want. But I am saying that this expanded definition is significantly more concrete, and thus more comprehensible and interesting, than just saying, "We should be respectful." The very name Word Picture means "paint a picture with your words—use your words to create a stimulating mental vision that allows the person hearing those words to know what it feels like to live them." And tough messages become so much easier to hear if our truth partner can figure out what we're actually saying.

Word Pictures in Action

Word Pictures can be built for practically any topic, and they can be used to discuss both performance issues and relationship issues. For example, you could build a Word Picture to help employees understand how they should and should not speak to customers, or what it really means to be more efficient, or what behaviors do and don't constitute good teamwork. All of those examples would be considered performance issues.

Alternatively, let's say you and a coworker are having a tough time getting along; you could build a Word Picture that describes what behaviors constitute a good or bad relationship. Or if you're about to have a tough conversation with a difficult client, you could build a Word Picture that establishes the ground rules for your conversation. Those would be considered relational Word Pictures.

Let's look at two different examples to see how we can use Word Pictures in a variety of situations, starting with a relational example.

Matt and Jane, executives at an insurance company, really don't like each other. Matt oversees IT, Jane runs claims, and for the past year they've done little besides engage in political battles, both passive-aggressively and aggressive-aggressively. In addition to a laundry list of legitimate operational grievances on both sides, their personalities are like oil and water. But last week, the CEO made clear that he is sick of the infighting and wants it to stop immediately. So Matt decides that it's time to figure out some way for him and Jane to work together.

Matt knows that at least a portion of their interpersonal problems stems from Financial Resistance; he and Jane have operational targets that are not aligned. But on a practical level, the CEO is not going to tolerate that as an excuse. Matt also sees that he and Jane are both affected by some Perceptual Resistance. While Jane is one of his internal customers, the level of service his department provides has been good enough in every other company at which he's worked. Matt wouldn't have imagined that another executive would see IT's role so differently, but if he really takes Jane's perspective, he can admit that he would probably be irritated, too. After all, when he thinks about specific times when he's felt annoyed by poor customer service, like from hardware vendors, he hasn't been at his calmest.

Thinking about the CEO's edict to stop the infighting, Matt knows that six months from now, he and Jane need to be working together in a demonstrably better way. He doesn't want to leave this company, and when he temporally distances himself from his current anger, he can see how it would be nice not to waste an hour every day on interpersonal fights. And really, while there's resistance on both sides, his goal here isn't terribly complicated; he and Jane just have to set some guidelines to work together more harmoniously.

Matt stops by Jane's office early in the morning and, using the IDEAS script, says, "Jane, I know this is going to sound a little weird, but would you be willing to have a conversation with me about how we can work together more effectively? I'd really like to get on the same page as you, and since we probably have different perspectives, I thought that we could discuss things and figure out a way to move forward together. Is that a conversation you'd be open to having?"

Jane looks at Matt somewhat skeptically and responds, "I think I'd be open to that. When do you propose we meet?"

They agree to meet for lunch, and when they meet at the restaurant later that day, Matt begins the conversation by saying, "I'm not sure what you're thinking, but I thought that rather than looking into the past and hashing out every fight we've ever had, maybe we could look forward and together map out what we'd like our working relationship to look like going forward."

"Go on," says Jane.

"Well, I was reading about this technique called Word Pictures, and basically what we would do is write down some concrete behaviors that exemplify a good working relationship, a bad working relationship, and then a great working relationship. We'd take turns, going back and forth, and when we get it done, we'd basically have a crystal clear map of exactly how we should be interacting with each other."

Jane looks a little confused. "Give me an example of what you're talking about," she says.

Matt has an example prepared, and it's one that casts him in a bad light. He figures that if he starts with an example that shows him messing up, Jane will be less defensive and maybe even reciprocate his openness. He says, "One of the first issues that I think makes for a good working relationship is responding well to work requests from a coworker." Matt knows that he has responded to many of Jane's IT requests with irritation, condescension, and even outright refusal. "I suppose that a bad response to a coworker's request would be reacting negatively or denying the request without even asking clarifying questions," Matt continues. "Or using negative language to describe the request, like saying it's stupid, dumb, or it doesn't make sense." He thinks for a minute and then says, "So I guess the good version would be asking clarifying questions to assess exactly what the coworker wants to achieve, and probably instead of negative language, the person should only speak factually."

"I definitely like where you're going so far," Jane says. "And in building on that good example, I think that a great example would be using the scripts I developed in the claims department. For example, always asking three clarifying questions when someone makes a request, always giving an answer within three hours, and using the statement 'I'm here to help meet your needs.'"

Matt immediately interprets Jane's examples as a dig at him, but he catches himself mentally straying from the facts. For a split second, he closes his eyes and, using self-distancing, imagines how a video camera might see this conversation. Matt realizes that Jane's comment probably wouldn't sound as bad to an outsider as it does to him, so with the FIRE Model firmly in mind, he resolves to focus exclusively on the facts, without interpretations or reactions. And one relevant fact is that he likes Jane's examples. Matt compliments Jane's examples and adds them to the list he's writing, and the conversation continues.

For 45 minutes they go back and forth, building this Word Picture. After solving coworker requests, they create examples for not gossiping, delivering good service, interacting in meetings, handling disagreements, and being respectful. When they're done, Jane looks at Matt and says, "I'll be honest, Matt. I don't know if either of us is going to be 100 percent in the good or great examples. And we've got a lot of teaching and coaching to do if we're going to get the folks on our staffs to buy into this. But I will admit that making these Word Pictures was a lot more productive than I thought. And if we can get something like this hashed out, we can probably fix lots of other issues as well."

Jane and Matt used Word Pictures to calmly and logically address their relational issue in a solutions-focused manner. Now let's look at Word Pictures in a performance example.

Sofia is a project management director at a pharmaceutical company and has been struggling mightily to get her employee, Lauren, to take on work that Lauren considers "outside her job description." Whenever Lauren is assigned one of these tasks, she rolls her eyes, scoffs, points a finger, crosses her arms, and has even stormed out the door. Sofia has been trying for six months to coach Lauren, but has achieved little success thus far.

Three days ago, the situation got ugly. After a contentious staff meeting, Sofia called Lauren into her office and told her, "Your negative attitude is not appreciated. You need to cut it out." As we'd expect, the meeting went downhill fast. Lauren started to cry and said, "This has never been on my performance review before, and there's no way I'm losing my job over this!"

During the conversation, and feeling the heat of angry emotions, Sofia briefly toyed with firing Lauren. But a little voice in her head said, "Your department is already understaffed," so Sofia instead ended the meeting before she lost her cool. Lauren left the meeting, and Sofia hashed over the situation, finally deciding to make one more attempt at fixing Lauren's performance. But this time she would approach it with more forethought and a better plan.

Sofia knows that Lauren is highly resistant to doing anything outside her putative role. Lauren is perceptually resistant to the idea that "helping others" is part of her job, while Sofia sees "helping others" as essential to life as breathing. Sofia also knows that, picturing the department six months from now, her best employees will quit if she doesn't get this issue fixed.

Sofia decides to try building a Word Picture, but she's going to get a bit creative. She knows that if she asks Lauren to have a one-on-one conversation, Lauren will just refuse. And even if she accepted the invitation, it's clear that Lauren has no problem making conversations contentious—and Sofia readily admits that she struggles to stay factual when Lauren is contentious. Sofia has also seen that Lauren behaves better in front of the other employees than she does one-on-one with just Sofia.

With these factors in mind, Sofia gathers all 10 of her employees into a meeting to create a Word Picture that defines teamwork for the department. Not only is Sofia's goal for this conversation fairly complex, especially given Lauren's willingness to make this fight public, but Lauren's resistance is so deep that Sofia doesn't think she can solve this without some help. Sofia feels that if she can get the majority of folks to define teamwork as including taking on work outside their own roles, she'll have created significant pressure on Lauren to improve or risk repercussions from her coworkers.

Sofia kicks off the meeting by saying, "Thank you all for being here today. The purpose of today's meeting is to create a Word Picture. In essence, we're going to collaboratively define how we should all work together in this department, aka teamwork. Let's start by going around the table and each of us give an example of what good teamwork looks like."

The first person to speak, Mike, says, "I just looked up teamwork on my phone, and *Webster*'s says that teamwork means 'work done by several associates with each doing a part but all subordinating personal prominence to the efficiency of the whole.' So how about we start with that?"

"That's great, Mike," Sophia says. "Does anyone have an example we can use, maybe starting with 'subordinating personal prominence to the efficiency of the whole'?"

Frannie, who is sitting next to Mike, says, "Last month I was struggling to run the new statistics software to produce the utilization report, and I had to present it in the morning. Joe didn't have to help me, but he stayed late and taught me the software. And even though he did a huge amount of work, he declined when I asked him to copresent with me, telling me he was just happy to help and didn't want any credit."

"That's brilliant," says Sofia. "And by the way, Joe, I think we should all applaud the example you set for us." After some actual applause, Sofia continues, "Without naming names here, can anyone describe what bad behaviors would represent a nonexample—you know, an example of bad teamwork?"

Mike jumps in, "How about complaining when you're given short notice for a project, or turning down requests when one of your coworkers asks for help. I think both of these are bad behaviors or nonexamples."

"And adding to that," says Joe, "I think not offering help without having to be asked is a nonexample."

Sophia is thrilled. The conversation is proceeding better than she had hoped. Lauren hasn't spoken up; she's just sitting there staring down at the table, but Sofia hadn't expected her to participate. But then, the group's dialogue takes an unexpected turn. Jill, who is sitting across the table from Lauren, says, "I've got a super-example. Last week Lauren was a huge help to me, and she probably didn't even realize it." As Jill speaks, Lauren looks up with discernible surprise.

"I was hugely pressed for time, and I was behind in getting my slideshow done for the companywide conference," Jill continues. "At one point I literally banged my head on my desk. Lauren heard me swearing and leaned over to ask if I was okay. After I explained my problem, she told me that she had a slideshow from last year's conference and I was welcome to use it. She told me where it was on the server and said all I had to do was replace the data. It was a lifesaver for me!"

Sofia's face was impassive, but inside she was stunned! Lauren was being quoted for an example of good teamwork? Sofia figured that Jill was just trying to be nice, but even so, it was a shocker. And then it got even stranger as Lauren spoke up. "Thanks Jill," she said, "it really wasn't a big deal. But I'm realizing that there have been numerous times that each of you has gone above-and-beyond to help me out. And I'm going to try to do more of those super-examples."

Not in her wildest dreams had Sofia considered the possibility that Lauren would have a light bulb moment. She figured that this Word Picture exercise would create social pressure on Lauren to act better, but she never imagined that Lauren would "see the light."

THE POWER OF UNIVERSALIZABILITY

Word Pictures define, explain, and elucidate. And when they're built collaboratively, as in the previous examples, they can create stunning moments of self-awareness. Word Pictures work so well because of concept attainment and concreteness, but there's one other mechanism that makes them successful: universalizability.

Imagine that I'm someone who speaks disrespectfully. I probably don't notice these behaviors in myself. But when I participate in creating a Word Picture, I'm not initially thinking about my own personal behaviors; I'm looking at whether certain behaviors should be held up as a universal standard to which everyone must adhere. I may not fully realize that I speak disrespectfully, but I can imagine someone else speaking disrespectfully to me. And I don't like that thought. So when I'm helping create a Word Picture, it makes perfect sense that I agree with a standard saying, "We speak factually and avoid negative emotion words like *angry, hate, sucks, stupid, moron,* etc." After all, I think that's a good universal rule.

It's not until after I agree to that universal example that a nagging voice starts to whisper in my brain, "Hey, dude, you remember that time you called your colleague stupid?" I can now start to feel some cognitive dissonance; I agreed to this universal example only to now realize that I've broken it myself on occasion. But it's too late to revoke my support for the example, so I do the only thing I can to reduce the dissonance, and that's to start adhering to the standard.

Do you remember Leon Festinger, the father of cognitive dissonance whom we met in Chapter 1 in our discussion of Truth-Killers? One of his graduate students, Elliot Aronson, went on to fame in his own right, and is ranked as one of the hundred most eminent psychologists of the twentieth century. The reason I bring him up is that Aronson conducted a series of experiments that reinforce the point I just made.[4]

In one such experiment, he looked at the showering time of college students in drought-stricken California.[5] In an ideal world, if you see that your local area is in the midst of a drought, and water restrictions are in force, you should minimally take shorter showers. (There's a lot more you could do, of course, but we're going to focus on an easy activity.)

Aronson sent researchers, posing as water conservationists, to stop students outside a gym shower room and ask them to put their names on a banner made to encourage others to take shorter showers. The control group was simply asked to promote taking shorter showers by signing the banner. But the students in the experimental group not only were asked to sign the banner; a researcher also asked them a series of questions about their past shower use. And that's where the cognitive dissonance comes in.

Just signing a banner in favor of shorter showers probably isn't enough to make you feel lots of cognitive dissonance. But when you sign the banner and then, thanks to a series of questions, realize that even though you support water conservation, you've actually been a selfish water hog, you're going to feel dissonance. In turn, that feeling of cognitive dissonance is so painful that you'll alter your behavior for the better. And that's what Aronson found.

The researchers secretly timed students' showers after they got done answering questions about their past shower use. Students in the experimental group (the ones who were asked about their past shower use) had an average shower time of 3.5 minutes, which was significantly shorter than that of the students in the control group who only signed the banner.

This is precisely what happens when you create a Word Picture with your coworkers outlining ideal teammate behaviors and then, in the course of a team meeting, realize that you've been a lousy teammate. You will want to ease that dissonance as quickly as possible—probably by acting like a better teammate.

YOU MAY NOT NEED THE NEXT TWO STEPS

The two chapters that follow teach critical skills for Truth Talks: listening and sharing facts. But as important as those skills are, you may find that you're able to successfully resolve your Truth Talk just by building a Word Picture. Of course, reading the remaining chapters will be beneficial to you, but for some Truth Talks, you may not need to employ their techniques.

Think back to Sofia and Lauren. Sofia tried for six months to coach Lauren, with little success. But in the course of one team meeting, building a Word Picture and using the power of universalizability to induce cognitive dissonance caused Lauren to have a "light bulb moment." The skies part, the choirs sing, and Lauren essentially says "Aha, I get it! I've been selfish and a poor teammate. But now I understand and I'm going to change my ways!"

I refer to this light bulb moment as making a "corrective leap." A corrective leap is that magical flash of insight during which we realize not only that we've been wrong, but what we've been doing wrong, why we were doing it wrong, and perhaps even how to do it right.

Lauren made a corrective leap during the team meeting; she put herself on a path to greatly improved performance. Sofia should keep monitoring and positively reinforcing Lauren's progress, but for all practical purposes, this Truth Talk is complete.

You too can engineer your Truth Talks and Word Pictures to spark the same kind of corrective leap that Lauren experienced. And it only takes two steps. First, build your Word Picture collaboratively. Second, once you've built and are looking at the Word Picture, ask your truth partner one of these questions: "How would you assess yourself on this Word Picture?" or "Can you think of times when you've done some of those nonexamples?"

However you ask the question, your goal, as in the shower study, is to generate some cognitive dissonance by having your truth partner compare the idealized Word Picture with his or her real-life performance. Some organizations do this as a regular part of their coaching, training, and onboarding.

For example, imagine that every month your organization creates a new Word Picture. Maybe in January you create a Word Picture about treating one another respectfully. Then in February you create a Word Picture describing customer service. March could be about teamwork, and so on. When you have these Word Pictures, you'll want to conduct a quick training for all the managers, so that they all understand the ins and outs of each one.

Once your managers are trained, you can send them out to have short, monthly conversations with each of their employees. Imagine that every leader has a one-on-one coaching session with each team member. And rather than saying, "Let me, the boss, evaluate your performance," the manager instead says, "How would you assess yourself on this Word Picture?" This develops employees' critical self-awareness, and because the Word Pictures are so concrete and loaded with examples, people immediately see where they should focus their personal improvement efforts.

Today's leaders talk a lot about wanting employees to be more proactive and accountable and to act on their own initiative. And yet those same leaders often turn around and say to employees, "I have to give you feedback; I have to evaluate your performance; I have to hold you accountable." This leaves employees, much like children, left to take feedback, to take evaluations, and to passively wait to be held accountable.

But better leaders are abandoning this style of parent-child leadership and replacing it with a new model of leadership that treats employees like adults who have unlimited potential and who deserve the opportunity to take control of their own futures. Establishing an adult-to-adult dynamic, rather than a parent-child one, encourages employees to become self-leading and self-sufficient, and results in a more motivated, fulfilled, and energized workforce, with greater accountability and better performance.

ONE FINAL THOUGHT

Years ago, I watched a television show about an NFL team during training camp—HBO's *Hard Knocks*. During one of the episodes, the third-string quarterback (who you just knew was going to get cut) asked the coach, "What can I do to get better?" To which the coach replied, "Just keep doing what you're doing."

The quarterback obviously didn't know what he should do differently, so he got frustrated with the coach's answer. He didn't articulate his frustration well, so here's a distillation of what he said: "What I'm currently doing has gotten me to be third-string! What should I do differently so that I can become second-string or even first-string?"

I recount this story because I see this same kind of scenario over and over again when I'm working with managers. "Keep doing what you're doing," they tell their people. To which any employee can justifiably respond, "Well gee, what I'm doing just got me put on a 90-day improvement plan, so have you got anything a little more specific to offer me?" Now you have something specific to offer your people. Word Pictures are the solution.

7

LISTEN WITH STRUCTURE

One of the critical skills you'll need to conduct a Truth Talk actually has nothing to do with talking; rather, it's all about listening. Once you've set your goals, invited a dialogue, and created a Word Picture, you're going to hit a point in the conversation where your truth partner will really start talking. People will share what's going on inside their head, reveal their interpretations, reactions, and ends, and basically tell you everything you should know to engage them effectively. The catch is that if you don't listen deeply, you'll never get any of that information. And without listening, you won't have a Truth Talk; you'll just have a reciprocated diatribe.

One of the most famous studies on listening comprehension was conducted years ago by Ralph Nichols, a rhetoric professor at the University of Minnesota. He studied hundreds of people and discovered something we intuitively already know; immediately after people have listened to someone talk, they generally remember only about half of what they heard, no matter how carefully they thought they were listening.[1]

Interestingly, great listening has little to do with our innate capability to retain information; it's much more about how we focus our mind, attend to our listener, and structure what we're hearing. If we develop our listening skills, not only do we gather more insight, but also our truth partner notices we're listening and thus shares more. This gives us even greater insight, and the virtuous cycle continues.

Salespeople with great listening skills sell more. Physicians with great listening skills face fewer malpractice lawsuits and have better patient outcomes. Leaders with great listening skills have more inspired and engaged employees. One of my studies found that one of the biggest drivers of employee engagement was whether employees felt that when they shared a work problem their boss listened and responded constructively. Alas, this same study also found that only about a third of leaders actually do listen and respond constructively. There's a pretty big listening deficit out there.

THIS IS WHAT "NOT LISTENING" SOUNDS LIKE

Scott is a vice president for a large manufacturer. The company recently conducted an employee survey and discovered that the frontline employees don't trust their supervisors. So Scott decides to conduct "skip level" meetings in which he'll meet with the frontline employees without the supervisors (who fall in between Scott and the employees on the org chart).

About 40 employees show up to the first meeting. Scott kicks things off by saying, "Welcome everybody. As you know, I'm having this meeting today because I want to hear your concerns directly. I'm here to listen about your issues with your supervisors, so fire away."

Tommy raises his hand first and says, "With the recent cost-cutting, I think we've all got concerns about whether we're going to have jobs next year."

Scott quickly responds, "Oh, I hear you. You think you've got problems? At least your wages are ones that other companies will pay. But I'm the VP and I'm over 50, so when you combine my high salary with my age, I'm going to have a really tough time finding a job. But hey, life's not fair, right?"

Sally chimes in next. "I actually have a different concern. My supervisor tells me that I'm supposed to bring him any suggestions for improvement, but when I do, it's like he doesn't listen to me."

Scott looks at her thoughtfully and says, "I know how that feels, but I don't want you to worry, because those feelings will pass and you will get over it."

Then Gail raises her hand and says, "My supervisor actually swore at me during my performance review, telling me my work was a pile of you-know-what."

"Yeah, that sounds bad," replies Scott. "But if there's one thing I've learned in my career, it's that griping about it won't make it better. Sometimes we've all just got to suck up tough feedback and move on with life. And you know what? I think that maybe it's a blessing in disguise."

Jim can sense that his coworkers are feeling angry and ignored, so he interjects, "I'm really concerned that this meeting isn't going to change anything because . . ."

"Let me stop you right there," Scott interrupts. "I know you're all feeling frustrated, and I get it. I really do. But we've all got our crosses to bear. So let's just focus on the positives and go out there and give our best effort."

Tommy, Sally, Gail, and Jim all spoke up, but Scott didn't listen to any of them.

SEVEN PHRASES THAT SAY "I'M NOT LISTENING"

I wish the above example was fictitious, but it's not. Examples of not listening can be found in virtually every office and home around the globe. You won't always find that many bad examples crammed into one situation, but it's pretty easy to find at least one or two.

Normally, I prefer to focus on what to do more than on what not to do, but there are seven phrases that are so commonly uttered, and that so clearly say, "I'm not listening," that I'd be remiss to let them pass without mention. You may not always hear the exact version listed below, but you've certainly heard some variation.

I'm Not Listening Phrase #1:
"Griping About It Won't Make It Better."

Telling people that whatever they're sharing is "just griping" is a sure-fire way to shutter any future conversations. When our VP Scott in the example above says, "I'm here to listen," the ideal action is for him to actually listen. He may not like everything that everyone tells him; however, he said he would listen. But when he says "griping about it won't make it better," he's essentially telling Gail that "what you just said was stupid and whiny and you should shut up." And that's not going to encourage others to tell him anything in the future.

I'm Not Listening Phrase #2: "Suck It Up."

Along the same lines, telling someone to "suck it up" says that "the thing you're telling me isn't even a real problem." In other words, if you were tougher (or a real man/woman), you wouldn't have noticed anything wrong to begin with.

I'm Not Listening Phrase #3: "Life Is Unfair."

This says that sure, bad stuff happens, and we all have some feelings about that, but I don't really care to hear about the bad things that are happening to you. Just accept that bad things happen and get on with your life.

I'm Not Listening Phrase #4:
"Maybe It's a Blessing in Disguise."

This is a wonderful rationalization that people use to excuse their complicity in tough situations. It basically says, "Yes, I threw you under the bus in that meeting last week, but rather than hearing your side of things, I'll just tell you to view this positively. If you can come to see this as a good thing, then I won't have to listen to you gripe about it." When Gail tells Scott about her supervisor's terrible behavior, Scott clearly doesn't want to listen. Instead, he wants Gail to see this as a blessing so he doesn't need to actually do anything.

I'm Not Listening Phrase #5:
"Don't Worry; You'll Get Over It."

Few phrases are as blatantly unempathic as this one. It's essentially saying, "You don't need to share your perspective with me because if you wait long enough, you'll just stop having any feelings about it." I once observed a training of psychiatry residents in which they were practicing empathic statements. They were presented with a fictitious mother whose child had just died, and they were instructed to say something conveying empathy. The resident I remember most clearly looked at the actor playing the mother and said, "Don't worry, it feels bad now, but you'll get over it." Hearing this made me feel sick.

I'm Not Listening Phrase #6:
"You Think You've Got Problems?"

Nothing says "I matter more than you" like turning someone else's moment of sharing into a narcissistic opportunity to vent all the frustrations you feel. When listening to someone else, we should actually be thinking about that person and what he or she is saying. So it's predictably terrible when we turn around and tell the person, "Hey, all that stuff you just said is unimportant, so I'm going to talk about myself now."

I'm Not Listening Phrase #7: "Yes, But . . ."

During one of my studies, I followed a number of executives through their workday to observe their communication skills. One guy I shadowed was such a terrible listener that I literally started counting the number of times he said, "Yes, but . . ." during one day of meetings and conversations. I stopped counting when I crossed 50. Perhaps more important than the frequency with which he uttered this phrase was the reaction of those around him. Each time he said "Yes, but," the conversation stopped dead. This executive claimed he wanted to listen, but as soon as people spoke to him, he'd shut them down.

INTERRUPTING IS ALSO BAD

In a landmark study on listening, or the lack thereof, professors Howard Beckman and Richard Frankel recorded and analyzed 74 patients' visits to the doctor. We've all been to the doctor for one reason or another, and ideally when the doctor enters the examination room, the first question asked should be something like "So what brings you in today?" In response, we should detail our full list of issues, and then the fancy medical stuff can get under way. But in reality, that's not how things actually work.

Of the 74 patient-doctor conversations, only 17 of the patients were able to complete their opening statement of concerns; that's about 23 percent. Why? In 51 of the visits (69 percent), the physician interrupted the patient's statement and directed questions toward a specific concern. And not only were the patients interrupted, but the interruptions occurred, on average, 18 seconds after they started to speak.[2]

Imagine a patient is sitting in the examination room and the doctor walks in and asks, "So what brings you in today?"

And the patient says, "Well, among other things, I've been having some headaches recently . . ."

"Tell me about the headaches," interrupts the doctor. It seems likely that the patient had some other issues she wanted to discuss, but once interrupted, she's unlikely to go back and finish her initial thoughts. In fact, in the Beckman-Frankel study, only one of the 51 interrupted patients was given a chance to go back and complete her opening statement.

A dozen years later, another group of researchers replicated this study. This time, out of 264 patient-physician interviews, 72 percent of patients were interrupted before completing their initial statement. And the interruptions occurred about 23 seconds after the patient started speaking.[3]

Here's a bit of irony: One of the common rationales that interrupters give is they're concerned that the speaker will ramble on for way too long. But in this study, when those few patients were allowed to complete what they wanted to say, they only took up an additional six seconds on average than the patients who were interrupted.[4] So letting people speak fully and complete their thoughts probably isn't going to take another 20 minutes. If this study is any indication, we're talking about a few more seconds.

We've all felt the temptation to interrupt. But when we do, it seriously hampers communication, ruins our reputation as "someone people can talk to," and typically infuriates the person who gets interrupted. Parenthetically, this reminds me of a knock-knock joke my kids used to tell.

Knock, knock.
Who's there?
Interrupting cow.
Interrupting cow wh—
MOOOOOOOOOO!!!!!!!!

Interruptions are annoying, don't you agree?

STRUCTURED LISTENING

Listening effectively requires a process that positively impacts the person speaking, gets us the appropriate information, and fully engages our brain. Here's a little tidbit that will make you think differently about listening: the average person can speak around 125 words per minute, but our brain can process about 400 words per minute.

In essence, our brain has lots of unused capacity when we're listening to someone speak. So what do most people do with that unused capacity? Well, it sure isn't listening even harder. Instead, most people get distracted by other thoughts, start skipping ahead to what they hope the speaker says, make their shopping list, or whatever. We need a structured process for listening. And not just because it gets us more and better information, but also because it keeps our brain engaged.

The process we're going to employ involves three parts: eliciting, listening, and confirming. Together, these three parts make up what I call Structured Listening.

Structured Listening Part 1: Eliciting

Eliciting is a process with which you're already familiar. It's essentially part of the IDEAS script we use to begin a Truth Talk. Note that if you're in the midst of a Truth Talk, and your truth partner is already sharing all sorts of interesting information, you can skip this step and move right on to the listening part.

Eliciting is where we communicate to our truth partner that we want to hear his thoughts and encourage him to share those thoughts. We do this by saying two things: the first is a statement, and the second is a question. Pairing the two, we'd say, "I'd really like to understand your perspective. Can we review the situation so I can get on the same page as you?"

The first utterance, the statement, tells our truth partner that we really do want to listen to him. And it serves as an important reminder to ourselves that we're entering a period of listening. The second utterance, the question, has two purposes. By asking "Can we review the situation . . . ," we're allowing the other person to agree to this conversation. As soon as he says yes, whether consciously or unconsciously, he becomes a more willing participant in this Truth Talk. This stops him from feeling like he's being subjected to these next steps, because he's agreeing to this dialogue.

The second part of this question, ". . . so I can get on the same page as you?," is a signal that we really want to listen to the person. We could have asked "so we can get on the same page?," but that doesn't have a particularly positive connotation. When we say "I want us to get on the same page" or "we need to get on the same page," we're really saying "I want you to get on the same page as me." And that isn't listening. Even if our intentions are pure and wonderful, the other person typically hears that he or she needs to be the one to listen to us.

So we reorder the language to flip the script and shatter the traditional framing that people associate with painful (and unproductive) conversations. I'm not going to order you to listen to me because you won't do it and the conversation will end badly. Instead, I'm going to listen to you (and if I do this well, eventually you'll reciprocate and listen to me).

You Can Tweak This Script

There are many different ways you can tweak the Eliciting script, as long as you convey the two central points: "I'd really like to understand your perspective. Can we review the situation so I can get on the same page as you?"

For example, imagine that you're a call center representative providing technical support for a computer company. Every day you take dozens (or hundreds) of calls from customers who are angry because the computer they bought isn't working as they expected. When your line buzzes, you could follow the procedure most call centers use and begin the conversation by asking something inane like "How are you today?" But if you're working in a call center to provide technical support, isn't it reasonable to assume that the customer didn't pull a Stevie Wonder and "just called to say I love you?" Seriously, when's the last time you called your computer, phone, cable, or credit card company support lines to express your happiness?

Because you know so much about perspective-taking, you understand the ridiculousness of starting a conversation with an angry person by asking, "How are you today?" You wouldn't say that if an angry coworker stormed into your office; it would only make her angrier. By contrast, if you wanted to calm that coworker, you could say, "I'd really like to understand your perspective. Can we review the situation so I can get on the same page as you?"

If you're working the phones in the call center, you might want to alter the script slightly, simply because you don't personally know the person on the other end of the phone. So you could say something like this example:

"Hi, my name is Mark. My job is to listen to you, gather some information, and then help you fix the computer's issues. So let's talk for a few minutes about the computer. Then we'll see if there's anything else you'd like to share, and then we'll perform some diagnostics. Does that sound okay?"

The original Eliciting script has been tweaked to fit our call center scenario, but it's still got the two essential elements: communicating how much you're interested in listening to the person's perspective and, with the question, getting her agreement to move forward.

There is a twist to this variation, however; the customer was told explicitly that they'd be talking for a few minutes. In the typical tough conversation with a coworker, employee, or boss, it's generally expected that this conversation is going to take a few minutes (at least). If I invite an employee into my office for a conversation, neither of us is particularly worried that we're not going to have sufficient time to express ourselves. We may worry about lots of other issues, but we're not concerned about being pressed for time.

But call centers, like physicians' offices, are venues in which we do worry about time pressures curtailing our conversation. So in this modified Eliciting script, we allay that fear by explicitly saying, "Let's talk for a few minutes . . ." By reducing the other person's anxiety, it encourages callers to share more information, and as a result, they feel considerably more "heard." And in case you were thinking back to the research I shared about interruptions in physicians' offices, yes, a modification like this would work very well there.

Structured Listening Part 2: Listening

The second step of the Structured Listening process is actually Listening. And this is the part where we keep our lips sealed, our ears open, and our brain active. And we're going to use the FIRE Model we learned in Chapter 2 to help bring structure to the conversation.

The bad news is that you might not be able to change the way people walk into your office and unload. In fact, more often than not, when someone is mad (or hurt, or scared, or most negative emotions), the rational brain is not fully engaged. The person's in fight-or-flight mode, and given that this person has stormed into your office to vent, it's a safe bet that you're dealing with fight mode. In this mode, you will typically hear an emotional, rambling list of frustrations—a list that is virtually certain to not be a structured and cogent argument.

The good news is that the FIRE Model will turn this disordered list of frustrations into a structured, cogent argument. You listen to what the person says, and as you're listening, you sort the utterances into one of the four buckets: Facts, Interpretations, Reactions, or Ends.

Figure 7.1   FIRE Model grid

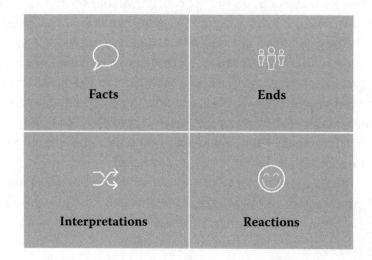

You're going to ask, "Do you mind if I take notes because I want to make sure I don't miss anything?" When the person says yes, take out a piece of paper and draw a two-by-two grid, like the one in Figure 7.1.

If you get the incredibly rare person (about one in a million) who says, "No, you can't take notes," just say, "May I ask why?" This typically elicits an emotional and angry response, for example, "We're not in a lawyer's office!" or "I just want you to listen to me!" Don't react emotionally to whatever is said. Just calmly say, "I just want to make sure that I really understand your perspective. Taking notes helps me remember and not miss anything." This should get you the okay to take notes. In the extremely unlikely event that this doesn't solve the problem, you can proceed without taking notes and do the next part in your head.

As you listen to what is being said, start sorting the words into the four buckets: **Facts**, **Interpretations**, **Reactions**, and **Ends**. For example, imagine that one of your coworkers, Pat, storms into your office and accuses you of not giving her credit for her work during a recent team meeting:

"I missed the team meeting last week, but Emerson was there, and she told me that when you were updating everyone about the report, you kept saying 'I did this' and 'I did that,' like how you decided to run the cool statistics. She said that you never mentioned me; well, she said you listed all the people on the team, but that no one would remember my name. I worked just as hard as you did on that report, and I feel like you really threw me under the bus. And if you really wanted all the credit, you should have just told me. And honestly, I wouldn't have put so much time and energy into the stupid report. Maybe I should just request to be off the team."

There's a lot going on in that blurb, including intense emotions and maybe a desire to quit the team, so let's examine Pat's remarks.

Are there any **Facts** in Pat's eyes? It's a fact that Pat had a conversation with Emerson. It's also a fact that Emerson did remember you mentioning everyone on the team. And for the sake of argument, let's assume that you did mention the names of everyone on the team equally, and you didn't single out any one person for additional recognition.

Pat just disgorged more than 100 words, and yet there are really only three facts. And while those facts may present an issue that requires resolution, those facts don't represent quite the four-alarm fire that Pat has brought into your office. Just as you saw in the previous chapter, when we dissect heated conversations and dislodge the Facts from the IRE, we often discover that the situation is nowhere as dramatic as it's presented initially.

What are Pat's **Interpretations**? Pat sees your equal mentions of everyone on the team as diminishing to her particular contributions. She sees it as being thrown under the bus. Pat also interprets this as you grabbing all the credit for the team's and her work.

Based on those Interpretations, is Pat experiencing any emotional **Reactions**? Indeed. Pat's reactions are mostly implied; she doesn't explicitly say "I'm angry" or "I'm feeling betrayed." But those sentiments are implied when Pat says "I feel like you really threw me under the bus" and "put so much time and energy into the stupid report." We'll explore this more in the next chapter, but when you hear emotionally loaded words like *stupid*, it's a sign you're probably hearing an emotional reaction.

And as a result of Pat's emotional Reactions, do you see any desired Ends? When Pat says "Maybe I should just request to be off the team," she's expressing two ends, one explicit, one implied. The explicit (possibly) desired end is to be off the team. The implied end, however, could be interpreted as "I want some satisfactory resolution to this situation." It's not yet clear if Pat wants an apology or more credit or something else, but when she caveats her explicit desired end with the word *maybe*, she's signaling that she's probably open to a different resolution.

While someone is speaking, don't interject, interrupt, or otherwise stop the flow. Just listen and take your notes. And when the persons does eventually stop speaking, count to three before you say anything. And I don't mean a quick one, two, three. I mean say in your head, "one supercalifragilisticexpialidocious, two supercalifragilisticexpialidocious, three supercalifragilisticexpialidocious." (If you have no idea what *supercalifragilisticexpialidocious* means, you might want to watch the movie *Mary Poppins*.)

The purpose of pausing for at least three seconds before you say anything is twofold. First, counting to three in such a slow manner encourages your truth partner to keep talking. People generally dislike silence, and believe it or not, three full seconds is a long time when nobody's saying anything. At least half the time, the other person will find the silence sufficiently uncomfortable and will start speaking again.

We want our truth partner's initial articulation to be as complete as possible because it gives us the maximum amount of information with which to work. The more people reveal about their perspectives, the more we discover potential misunderstandings, and issues like cognitive dissonance and selective perception.

Also, many people feel a bit of catharsis as they keep speaking, or they just burn off some negative emotions (much like pro athletes start big games a bit jittery but settle down as they start running and utilizing that energy). Put yourself in the shoes of people who are so nervous about this conversation that they must pump themselves up to even walk down the hallway and cross the threshold into your office. Maybe they gave themselves a little pep talk in the mirror. Or slammed back an energy drink. Either way, they're amped up as they start speaking, and it's likely to take a few minutes of letting words come out (while you react calmly) for this nervous energy to ebb.

The second purpose of this slow three-count is to allow us time to de-escalate our own emotions and respond in a calm and measured way. The older part of our brain, the brain stem, rules the most basic human drives ("fight, flight, food, and fornication"). As you might guess, it's a powerful part of the brain. If this area is highly activated, other more evolved areas of the brain will take a backseat. Simply put, if we let ourselves get really worked up by what Pat just said, we aren't going to do a lot of higher-level reasoning.

And that's why we do our slow three-count. We don't want to get caught up in Pat's IRE; it's stimulating the wrong area of the brain. It's reinforcing the older brain stem (sometimes called the lizard brain), and it prevents us from accessing the more mammalian areas of the brain, where we do our higher-level thinking.

So when we pause, we slow our brain down. And rather than getting worked up by Pat's IRE, we need to focus on less emotional issues. Like listening analytically to sort everything Pat says into the four buckets of Facts, Interpretations, Reactions, and Ends. In neurochemical terms, it's about moving from adrenalin (tied to the fight-or-flight reaction) to oxytocin production, which triggers a more relaxed, supported, state—a "humanized" state.

Once in a while people will be so worked up when they start talking that you need to help them calm down. You could say, "Just calm down," but that's more likely to make people angry than calm. Instead, exhale like you're surprised by their intensity and say, "Wow, that's a lot to take in . . . give me a second." This is a subtle signal that tells people that they're coming on too strong or have gone too far. If you react like a scolding parent and yell at them to calm down, they'll respond like a petulant child and get even more worked up. But if you look a little stunned, exhale, and say, "Wow . . . ," they start to think, "Oh-oh, I came on too strong. I'd better tone it down a bit."

Structured Listening Part 3: Confirming

The third step in Structured Listening is Confirming. This is when we corroborate that we understood the other person correctly.

First we signal that we're going to say what we heard, then we'll use the FIRE Model to transpose what the other person said into something more structured and cogent, and finally we'll confirm that we got it right. In the case of our conversation with Pat, it might sound something like this:

> [Opening line] I want to make sure I really understand what you're saying.
>
> [Facts] You had a conversation with Emerson. Emerson said that I mentioned everyone on the team equally and did not single out any one person for additional recognition.
>
> [Interpretations] You took this to mean that I was diminishing your particular contributions and throwing you under the bus. You also took this to mean that I was grabbing all the credit for the team's and your work.
>
> [Reactions] Based on that interpretation, you're feeling like I threw you under the bus and maybe even angry and betrayed.
>
> [Ends] And as a result you're now thinking that maybe you should just request to be off the team.
>
> [Closing line] Did I get that right?

The opening line is very simple, but it delivers two clear messages. First, it says "I'm taking your perspective and I really want to understand what you have to say." It also says "You're not talking to an amateur . . . if we're going to have this conversation, we're going to have a thoughtful, mature, well-reasoned discussion using our brains."

The next step transforms Pat's jumbled words into a series of structured thoughts that proceed in a logical order. You're not doing this to one-up the person or to point and laugh. Your goal is to confirm that you accurately understood what she said. And it's a lot easier to understand what she's said when you have a methodology for accurate listening.

Another benefit to using this FIRE Model is that you can more accurately see the size and seriousness of the issue. And not only can you see more clearly; your truth partner can see more clearly as well. When Pat walked into the office and blurted her initial volley, it sounded like a serious interpersonal rift replete with betrayal, anger, and quitting. But when we dissect it, the situation doesn't seem quite so serious. And it's quickly evident that this situation is light on facts but heavy on interpretations, reactions, and ends (with a dose of hearsay for good measure).

When you add some structure to people's grievances, they often start to realize that they've blown things out of proportion. We haven't in any way minimized Pat's (or anyone's) concerns; we've simply repeated her words back with structure and logic. Consider, for example, when Pat says, "I worked just as hard as you did on that report, and I feel like you really threw me under the bus." That's serious stuff. But what if we say to Pat: "You had a conversation with Emerson. Emerson said that I mentioned everyone on the team equally and did not single out any one person for additional recognition. You took this to mean that I was diminishing your particular contributions and throwing you under the bus."

When Pat sees laid bare the train of thought that led her into your office, she's likely to realize that her reaction was disproportionately intense. So it's typical for someone in Pat's shoes to start moderating her emotions and perhaps even backtrack a little.

Ironically, while this chapter is putatively about listening (and us taking Pat's perspective), the act of making Pat's perspective more cogent exposes thinking errors or emotional escalations of which Pat wasn't aware. Our efforts are educating both ourselves and Pat about what Pat is really thinking. We're not doing therapy per se, but many a patient has entered therapy simply to gain a deeper understanding of his or her own thoughts and feelings.

The final piece of Confirming is asking Pat, "Did I get that right?" This is Pat's chance to say either yes, as is common if we've listened and confirmed accurately, or no. If Pat says no, she'll quickly follow up with ". . . and here's what you got wrong." You'll need to listen once more, incorporate the corrections, and again articulate what you heard using the FIRE Model.

Having to cycle through this once, twice, or even thrice is not indicative of failure. In fact, it demonstrates your commitment to deeply understand your truth partner's perspective. Ironically, the most profound rapprochements often come from conversations where more than one cycle was required for a party to agree that his or her perspective was taken accurately.

STRUCTURED LISTENING RECAP

Structured Listening gives you a methodology for seeing the world through someone else's eyes. A shocking number of disagreements can be resolved simply by proceeding step-by-step through the Structured Listening process.

Looking back at our situation with Pat, there's a very good chance that we solved the problem just by taking her perspective and reflecting it back using the FIRE Model. Once you get the IRE out of the way, we're left with a case of either Pat realizing that she overreacted and sheepishly backtracking or our explicitly recognizing Pat's contributions to the team (assuming that's warranted). At a minimum, Structured Listening makes seemingly insurmountable chasms of understanding seem resolvable. And the maximum outcome is that Structured Listening achieves a full resolution.

Also, having gone through a detailed Structured Listening process, I should have ample evidence to discover any of the Truth-Killers that might be influencing Pat's perspective. Is there anything about what I said at that meeting last week that might create cognitive dissonance? What about Selective Perception? Or Financial Resistance? Is there a truth in here that's incredibly hard to hear? Is Pat experiencing any Confident Unawareness?

Structured Listening is the process that reveals what's happening inside Pat's head. Once we have that data, discovering any psychological or logical impediments (aka Truth-Killers) is a very simple task. And in the event that Structured Listening didn't fully resolve the issue at hand, we'll need this extra bit of insight as we further our Truth Talk.

WHAT IF THE OTHER PERSON TALKS TOO MUCH?

As I noted earlier in the chapter, it's not uncommon for people to fear being stuck listening to someone who just won't stop talking. The evidence is pretty clear that this fear is overblown, but it's reassuring to know that there is a way to handle the rambling and excessive talker (just in case).

The first point I want to emphasize is that we shouldn't consider someone's talking as an issue if we're receiving useful information. Just because someone talks a lot doesn't mean it's rambling or excessive talking. If we're learning how people think, digging into specifics, and seeing their perspective more clearly, then it's important for us to keep listening. But there may come a point when they've exhausted any useful information and now we're just getting filler. In those cases, we can use the following technique.

Let's assume that we're talking to a rambling, excessive talker. He's given us great insight, but now he's rambling about who-knows-what. We don't want to rudely interrupt or accuse him of not making sense; so instead, we're going to use something he just said to get him back on track. Imagine that our talker started out describing a difficult team meeting at the last company retreat in New Orleans. But now he's descended into rambling about crawfish.

"I was working on this team, and let me tell you about this team; we used to meet in New Orleans, and New Orleans, man I never had a crawfish before. You know I used to pronounce it New Orleans, but then I learned it's 'Nawlins.' And man, it was just cool; I don't know, I was there one time right on Fat Tuesday, and right before Mardi Gras, oh my gosh, the parties then, and the crawfish, I mean it's like a lobster, and . . ."

Okay, that's legitimately a rambling mess. So we're going to take a piece of what he just said, paraphrase, and redirect it. For example, we might jump in and say, "Oh, so the team meeting was in New

Orleans—tell me about how it went." Or we could say, "It sounds like the team meeting had great food; tell me more about what was on the agenda there." We simply take a piece of what the person just said, paraphrase it, and then redirect the conversation.

If you interrupt and say, "Oh my gosh, I don't care about the crawfish; believe it or not, I've had crawfish before. Could we please get back on topic?," it sounds rude, and rudeness is likely to stifle any further conversation. Instead, we're being subtle about our redirection. We evidence that we've heard what the person said, and while it's interesting, there are other interesting topics we also need to discuss.

WHAT IF THE OTHER PERSON DOESN'T TALK ENOUGH?

Sometimes you'll have the opposite challenge, a conversation with someone who is reticent to speak. And when you're really committed to listening, it can be a little frustrating when the person is not saying enough for you to use your new skills. In those situations, you will have to do some probing and gather more facts. A good heuristic for gathering more facts comes from the poet Rudyard Kipling, who wrote:

> I keep six honest serving-men
>
> (They taught me all I knew);
>
> Their names are What and Why and When
>
> And How and Where and Who

Let's take a look at how it works:

Sally is an HR manager at a large hospital. One of the nurses, Tamara, is engaged in a conflict with a prominent physician, Dr. Jones, and Sally has been asked to do some digging. Sally calls Tamara into her office and says, "Regarding the issue with Dr. Jones, I'd really like to understand your perspective. Can we review the situation so I can get on the same page as you?" Tamara replies, "Well, I had a conflict with Dr. Jones last week."

Sally pauses a full three seconds, but Tamara offers nothing further. Sally knows she doesn't have any of the "who, what, when, where, why, and how," so she probes a little: "What happened as a result of that conflict?"

Tamara answers, "Well, it was actually two conflicts, if I'm being totally honest here, and you know, we had this conflict, and after one of them a medical error occurred."

Uh-oh, Sally thinks to herself. Still lacking sufficient detail, she probes a bit more: "So you had these two conflicts with Dr. Jones, and as a result, the medical error occurred. I'm wondering, did anybody else have conflicts with Dr. Jones?"

"Well, no, you know that's what was really weird," Tamara says. "Nobody else really had a conflict with Dr. Jones; I'm the only one, and you know, he's been here for 10 years."

There's a lot more probing that Sally could do, but you can see how this process works. When we're faced with someone who's just not supplying enough detail about the facts, we're likely going to have to ask some probing questions to reveal the "who, what, when, where, why, and how."

WHAT IF YOU'RE TRYING TO LISTEN IN A MEETING?

Have you ever been in one of those team meetings, virtual or face-to-face, where a few big personalities just dominate the space? They usually talk louder than everyone else, and if the boss or team leader isn't speaking, all you hear are their thoughts, their ideas, their yeas and their nays. The quieter, more passive folks in the meeting feel shut out from participating, and even the people who usually don't have a problem being heard can't get a word in.

Unless you're the loud one who's stealing the show, you walk out of those meetings feeling anxious about the loss of your time, bitter that your good ideas didn't have a chance at getting heard, and irritated at the leader of the meeting for letting it happen. Is it any wonder that bad meetings can be so damaging to a leader's reputation?

Meetings are supposed to be value-adding forums where everyone invited to the meeting gets to participate. Isn't that why you called all those people into the meeting in the first place—to gather and apply their input and knowledge toward making smarter and better decisions?

The Nominal Group Technique for Meetings

The nominal group technique is designed to equalize every voice on the team. It's an intelligent approach to encouraging the quiet people to speak out while subtly pressuring the loud people to tone it down a bit. All the technique requires is you as the leader of the team exerting a bit more control over the group, which, after all, is just doing your job.

Let's say the team has a decision to make. The meeting agenda that went out to everyone says the purpose of this meeting is to debate and decide upon the proposal price for the new project we're pitching ACME Corp. You invited seven people to the meeting, and each person brings a unique and valuable perspective to making this decision. You need to hear what each of them has to say.

Here's how the nominal group technique works so you get to hear all those perspectives. As soon as everyone arrives at the meeting and settles down, pass around some sheets of paper, or if it's a virtual meeting, use a web meeting tool that allows people to write in responses. Then give these directions: "We're going to take five minutes here, and what I want is to get your individual ideas about how you think we should price this proposal. I want the number, but I also want to hear why you think it's the right number, so back it up with some pros and cons, the whys and the why nots, etc. You have five minutes to write it down, and then we're going to pass the papers to me to be discussed."

The nominal group technique quickly and easily accomplishes three big things. One, it forces everyone to take a step back and actually do some thinking. This applies especially to those loud voices I mentioned earlier who often just shout out the first idea that pops into their mind, thereby commandeering the meeting. Two, the nominal group technique gives every voice in the meeting an equal chance to be heard. And three, once everyone's ideas and thoughts are written down and passed over to you, you now have the opportunity to control the discussion that takes place in this meeting.

One way you can do this is to go through those pieces of paper one at a time and say, "Let me talk about this first idea. This person feels the contract should be priced at $12.5 million, which is $2.5 million higher than we usually charge for this job, but this person supports this higher number based on the tight timeline we're facing on this job, which is going to mean more manpower focused away from other work." Then you move on to the second piece of paper and say, "This person feels $8.5 million is the right pricing for the job and points out that this sounds pretty lowball until you factor in the following numbers that outline the additional business this new client will likely bring our way." And so on until you hit on everyone's ideas.

Another approach, instead of having people write their ideas, is to start the meeting by saying, "I'm going to give every person here three minutes, with no interruptions from anyone, to share with the team your thoughts on how you think we should price this proposal and why." And again, in doing this, you immediately make everybody on the team more thoughtful. The people who might be inclined to shout out with knee-jerk responses are forced to tone it down, and the folks who may be inclined to passively hang back are forced to stand up and say, "Here is what I'm thinking."

ONE FINAL NOTE: NO PHUBBING

This is something I wish I didn't have to say, but I do, so here goes: When you're listening to someone, actually pay attention. And that means put down your phone! Phubbing is the act of snubbing people by looking at your phone instead of paying attention to them. It's a weird word, but you'll remember it if you think of it as meaning *ph*one-sn*ubbing*. I know, for some people, this doesn't seem like a big deal. And I'm not going to litigate generational issues at the end of a chapter. So I will simply say that there's ample evidence that, neurologically, multitasking is a myth; we really cannot give equal attention to two different tasks. That means that when we're touching or checking our phone, we're not truly engaged with the person with whom we're conversing. And for many folks, myself included, it is incredibly irritating to be phubbed.

James A. Roberts, a professor of marketing at Baylor University, coauthored a study on phubbing, published in the journal *Computers in Human Behavior*.[5] What he found should tell us everything we need to know: For people in relationships, more than 46 percent said their partners phubbed them. And of those who were phubbed, nearly 23 percent said it caused issues in their relationship. So please, put down your phone and listen.

8

SHARE
THE FACTS

Before we jump into this last piece of our Truth Talk, let's quickly review what we've accomplished so far. We began by familiarizing ourselves with the four Truth-Killers. We know that we can't just walk into someone's office and blurt whatever's on our mind. If we do, there's a good chance the person will experience Psychological Resistance, Perceptual Resistance, Financial Resistance, and/or Confident Unawareness and our words will go unheard. Knowing the potential obstacles we face, we then used the FIRE Model to separate our Facts from our Interpretations, Reactions, and desired Ends. By extricating the truth (Facts) from the IRE, we made our message more accurate and more palatable.

Next we took our truth partner's perspective by putting ourselves inside the person's head to learn how likely he or she is to receive our message. Armed with a factual message and a deep understanding of the person's likely acceptance (or resistance), we established a goal for our Truth Talk. By envisioning our future selves, we discovered the appropriate strategy for our talk, given the depth of likely resistance and the complexity of our goals.

With the prep work done, we began the actual conversation. We invited our truth partner into a conversation by asking, "Would you be willing to have a conversation with me? I'd like to review the situation to make sure I'm on the same page as you. And if we have different perspectives, we can discuss those and develop a plan for moving forward. Does that sound okay to you?" With our truth partner's agreement and conversational partnership, we collaboratively created a Word Picture. We used concrete language and nonexamples, examples, and super-examples to create stunning moments of self-awareness and agreement. In many cases, collaborating on Word Pictures will solve and conclude our Truth Talk. In the event that the Word Picture wasn't enough, we then asked our truth partner to share his or her thoughts. We used Structured Listening to dissever the person's thoughts into Facts, Interpretations, Reactions, and Ends. And in doing so, we identified any areas of disagreement and resistance.

With everything we've accomplished thus far, there's really only one thing left to do, and that's share our facts.

STRIP AWAY THE IRE

The FIRE Model taught us that we humans generally analyze our surrounding world via a four-step process. We notice some Facts, then we make Interpretations, about those facts, then based on our interpretations, we experience emotional Reactions, and once we experience those emotions, we have some desired Ends. Collectively, Facts, Interpretations, Reactions, and Ends form the FIRE Model. Before we start sharing our facts, we need to employ the FIRE Model and strip away everything that isn't a fact.

Let's revisit a previous scenario. Taylor manages the tech support department, and one of her employees, Hunter, hasn't been filling out his programming requests correctly. Taylor stops by his desk and says, "Hey Hunter, I noticed you're not filling out the error logs in your programming requests. We need to do that for reporting purposes. Can you take a look at your requests?" Hunter replies, "Oh, yeah, I keep forgetting about it; sorry. I'll update my open ones. I'll try to keep it in mind." Taylor says thanks and walks away.

A week goes by and nothing has changed. Once again, Taylor stops by Hunter's desk and says, "Hey Hunter, I noticed you're not filling out the error logs in your programming requests. We need to do that for reporting purposes. Can you take a look at your requests?" This time Hunter huffily replies, "These rules change all the time. How do you expect us to keep up? Like I've got nothing else to do but random data entry, just because the programmers can't look up the error logs themselves. But okay, fine. I guess I'll put all my real work on hold for the afternoon so I can report on work that's already done."

Did Taylor do anything egregiously wrong that would have triggered Hunter to respond this way? Compared with other cases we've evaluated, what Taylor said actually wasn't too awful. But even though Taylor's words weren't terrible, her comments to Hunter were not 100 percent fact based.

Let's compare two versions. First, here's what Taylor actually said: "Hey Hunter, I noticed you're not filling out the error logs in your programming requests. We need to do that for reporting purposes. Can you take a look at your requests?" In the second version, let's strip away absolutely everything that isn't a fact: "The error logs in your programming requests are not completed."

When we compare these two versions, the second, factual example feels more important than what Taylor actually said. That's because Taylor's comments contain a number of soft-pedaling words and phrases that diminish the importance of her directive. First, there's the casually friendly intro of "Hey Hunter," which makes this feel like chitchat rather than something more serious and job-related. Second, Taylor says, "I noticed . . . ," which implies that she just stumbled upon this issue. But she didn't just stumble upon the missing error logs; she's a manager and part of her fiduciary responsibility is ensuring completion of those logs. Third, Taylor asks Hunter ". . . can you take a look at your requests?" This connotes that the error logs are somehow optional.

The second version: "The error logs in your programming requests are not completed," is a clean and simple statement of fact. And because it's just the facts, without any soft-pedaling, the words carry more weight and importance. Now, it's entirely possible that even if Taylor had said this factual statement, Hunter could look at her and reply "So what?" In that case, Taylor would have to follow up with yet another statement of fact, namely, "Completing those error logs is a condition of continued employment."

Occasionally people will resist being so factual. They tell me, "Those facts just seem so cold. I'd rather make this more of a conversation." And I have to remind them where we are in the process of our Truth Talk. We've engaged in conversation, we've built Word Pictures, we've taken the person's perspective, and much more. If we've gotten to the point where Hunter hasn't yet made a corrective leap, it's time for us to deliver the facts.

Pretend that Taylor delivered the factual version instead, saying to Hunter, "The error logs in your programming requests are not completed." In saying this, Taylor isn't angry, threatening, emotional, or otherwise inflammatory. When Taylor sticks to the facts, she allows Hunter the freedom to choose his path. She's treating him like an autonomous, freethinking adult who owns the choice as to whether he's going to pursue corrective action. It's like telling someone "It's raining outside," which leaves it completely up to that person to make an adult decision about what to do with that information.

By contrast, when Taylor soft-pedals her message, she's engaging Hunter in more of a parent-child mode. It's like telling someone, "Hey, I just noticed it's raining outside; maybe you should think about a raincoat," which has a distinctly parent-child vibe.

Had Taylor followed the Truth Talk process from the outset, it's probable that she and Hunter would never have reached this point. Most likely the Word Pictures would have resolved the incomplete error logs. But we are at this point, so we need to share the facts. And more important, we need our truth partner to hear those facts. Because as you'll see in the next two sections, once the person hears the facts, we've got a final part of our Truth Talk we need to address.

THE POWER OF THE CORRECTIVE LEAP

We learned in the chapter on Word Pictures that a "corrective leap" is that magical flash of insight during which we realize that we've been wrong and recognize what we've been doing wrong, why we were doing it wrong, and perhaps even how to do it right. It's an important concept, because when we're sharing facts, we want to share just enough to ensure that our truth partner makes a corrective leap.

Lola and Violet are account managers and colleagues. Last week they met with one of their company's biggest clients, the Johnson account. Lola acquitted herself well in the meeting, but Violet made mistakes; she was angry and frustrated, and she let it show in her words and demeanor. Lola has a Truth Talk with Violet, and when she gets to the fact-sharing part, she says, "In the Johnson account meeting last week, there were three comments that you made that, when the client heard those comments, he got angry and red-faced. Do you know which comments I'm talking about?"

When Lola asks Violet, "Do you know which comments I'm talking about?," she's testing to see whether Violet has already made a corrective leap. It's entirely possible that Violet left that meeting thinking, "Wow, I messed that up. I never should have said those things. I need to control my anger better in the future." If Violet has made a corrective leap, there's no point in Lola piling on. In fact, if Lola does pile on, adding fact after fact after fact, she's likely to make Violet incredibly resistant.

The corrective leap signals that you don't need to spend the next 20 minutes detailing every single thing that person did wrong. She already gets it. It would be like talking to a star NFL quarterback who just threw a bad pass that was tipped and intercepted. If your quarterback is elite, and you say to him, "You know that was a bad pass, right?," he's likely to respond, "Ugh, yes. I know. I threw it off my back foot. I was on the run. I didn't plant my feet." That's a corrective leap, and hearing it indicates that you don't need to spend the next 10 minutes saying, "You know you didn't plant your feet, right?"

If someone has made a corrective leap, and yet we continue to berate that person with the facts, we're no longer engaged in a dialogue. For example, this is not a dialogue:

Coach: "You know you didn't plant your feet, right?"
Quarterback: "I just said I didn't plant my feet. Of course, I know I didn't plant my feet. It was stupid. I made a mistake."

>Coach: "Well, it was kind of stupid and you threw off your back foot."
>
>Quarterback: "Yeah, I know. I told you all of this."

It sounds cartoonish when I write it out like this, but the sad truth is that situations like this happen all the time. Someone enters a tough conversation with a script that says "Here's all the feedback I need to give." And he gives it, and gives it, and gives it, until every single point on the page has been hit. But that doesn't work. We only want to share enough facts to turn on the light bulb and achieve that corrective leap.

In the case of Lola and Violet, Lola needs to share enough facts for Violet to make a corrective leap. If Lola shares her first set of facts and Violet hasn't made a corrective leap, then Lola needs to share a few more facts and test again. If Lola says, "Do you know what comments I'm talking about in the Johnson account meeting?" and Violet says, "No, I have no idea. I thought I did a great job," then clearly Violet hasn't made a corrective leap. Lola will need to share a few more facts.

Perhaps Lola says, "Okay, let me give you an example. How about when you told the client that he was stupid for wanting his brochures printed in blue." With this additional fact, Violet is likely to have that light bulb moment and say, "Ugh, yes. Okay, I know exactly what you're talking about."

MOVING FORWARD TOGETHER

There's a reason we need our truth partner to make a corrective leap. Once the person's light bulb is on, we can then say, "Let's talk about how we can make things better in the future." The most enjoyable part of a Truth Talk isn't sharing facts; it's discussing how to move forward, when we brainstorm, problem-solve, and otherwise plot a positive future. Far too many difficult conversations get stuck in looking backward, discussing ad nauseam all the things that went wrong. While it takes some looking backward to create a corrective leap, ideally we're going to spend the bulk of our time looking forward and designing a better future.

Remember back in the Introduction when I said that a Truth Talk should create change? This is critically important. We're not having a Truth Talk if we're not focused on effecting change and making a better future. I can berate someone all day long, but that's not a Truth Talk. This conversation is only effective if we're able to create change.

It can be anticlimactic to think that our Truth Talk ends with a statement as seemingly mundane as "Let's talk about how we can make things better in the future." But remember, this statement wouldn't feel mundane if we hadn't taken every prior step. It's a testament to our having performed every previous step correctly that we're now able to engage in a positive and forward-looking discussion.

WHAT IF YOUR TRUTH PARTNER WON'T ACCEPT RESPONSIBILITY FOR THE FACTS?

Sometimes when people mess up, they dodge accountability and shift the responsibility to someone else. This is called blame. Maybe, for example, you've experienced someone who missed a deadline and then tried to throw a colleague under the bus by saying, "I couldn't get the report done on time because of Bob in Accounting. Bob never gives me the data on time, and that's the reason my report was late. How can I be expected to get the report done on time when Bob is always holding up my data?"

It's one thing to make an excuse like "the Internet crashed," which points fingers at an inanimate object. But it's quite another to cast aspersions about another person (or group of people). Those "other people" will learn of the blame, hurt feelings will abound, the blame may be reciprocated, and on it goes.

We all mess up from time to time, but blaming others for our mistakes is not a healthy or responsible coping mechanism. Blame is aggressive and attacking, and it's highly contagious. When people blame, they're basically trying to shift attention away from themselves. They're saying, "Don't look at me. Look at that other person." They do this to escape being pinned down for whatever mistake they made.

It's similar to a magician distracting the audience so he can maneuver the trick somewhere else. Blamers are typically quite good at derailing conversations and sending them in another direction. Let's imagine your employee Pat is late with a report. You call Pat into your office and have this brief dialogue:

> Boss: "Pat, the report I needed from you is past deadline."
> Pat: "Well, I can't possibly control that because Bob in Accounting didn't give me the numbers I needed to finish the report."

If Pat's line is said with enough intensity, many bosses will get sucked into a conversation about Bob and how Bob didn't get the numbers, or the Accounting department, or whatever. And this allows Pat to sidestep any real accountability. Pat may escape a conversation about why she didn't inform the boss of this problem sooner, or why she didn't work more effectively with Bob, or why she didn't submit the other parts of the report, etc. And all of those topics are more actionable than griping about Bob and the Accounting department.

When employees blame each other, it's up to the leaders to turn that blame into accountability. This requires using six simple words: "Let's discuss what we *can* control." Let's use these six words to redo the conversation between Pat and the boss:

> Boss: "Pat, the report I needed from you is past deadline."
> Pat: "Well, I can't possibly control that because Bob in Accounting didn't give me the numbers I needed to finish the report."
> Boss: "Okay, I hear that, but I don't want to talk about Bob. Let's discuss what we *can* control.
> Pat: "I told you, I don't control anything. It's Bob's fault, not mine."
> Boss: "Listen, I don't want to talk about Bob. Let's discuss what we *can* control. I don't want to talk about anybody else. I don't want to talk about anything outside of our control. And right now, there are things we control. We control our reactions; we control certain parts of the reports, etc."

In this scenario, by directing (and redirecting) the conversation back to the central issue: what you *can* control, it prevents Pat from dodging accountability. It's not a vicious reprimand, but rather a simple statement that says, "We're not changing topics; we're not discussing other people; we're only talking about what we *can* control."

By preventing the conversation from veering off track into an emotional blame game, Pat is forced to start taking ownership. The conversation moves away from fixing blame and onto fixing the issue.

Talking about issues we don't control is, by definition, an exercise in futility. If we don't control something, what's the point of spending the next 30 minutes griping about it? We may as well gripe about the weather; it's a waste of time and has absolutely no bearing on the weather. But when we keep redirecting the conversation back to issues we actually do control, we teach people that there is something controllable in every situation. And that, in turn, improves their accountability.

THE SOFTNESS PROBLEM

Now that we've covered how to share the facts, let's take a step back and discuss one of the challenges people face when sharing the facts: being so soft that we obfuscate the truth. There's significant pressure in today's organizations for everyone to be engaged, be inspired, have fun, and be fulfilled. And that's a great thing (who doesn't want work to be fulfilling?). But one of the potential unintended consequences of that pressure is that our conversations become so focused on making people happy that we forget to speak the truth and help one another be more effective.

Here are four signs that your interpersonal style may have become too soft, and thus insufficiently truthful.

Sign #1 That You're Too Soft: A 5-Minute Conversation Turns into 50 Minutes

Imagine you give an employee a highly specific bit of constructive feedback, for example, "This report is too long; shave off 1,000 words." The only response you really want is "I've got it. I'll fix it now." But imagine that even though this feedback conversation should be done within five minutes, you find yourself engaged in a lengthy conversation with the employee about why he fell short, how that makes him feel, and why you're somehow to blame for his mistakes.

Has that ever happened to you? If so, it's a sign that you've become too appeasing. It's good to encourage dialogue with your employees, and it's great when they feel comfortable sharing. But when employees believe they can talk themselves out of being criticized or held accountable, that's a problem.

There are times when someone just needs to say, "I'm sorry. I messed up. I'll fix it immediately." That's not indicative of a dictatorial environment; it's usually just a sign of efficiency and accountability. There are some conversations that should be five minutes and done. So when you regularly feel like 5-minute conversations are turning into 50-minute rambling sessions, that's a strong sign that you've moved from approachable to acquiescent.

Sign #2 That You're Too Soft: Your Meetings Get Off Topic and Take Too Long

Have you ever been in one of those meetings where one or two big personalities dominate the conversation? They talk louder than everyone else, and all you hear are their thoughts and ideas. And even when you try to rein them in, they manage to barge right through and keep dominating the conversation, sometimes even leading it astray.

Meetings are meant to be value-adding forums where all invitees participate. Yet when we struggle to control one or more individuals who don't respect others, it's a sign that we're not being assertive enough. Of course people should talk. Intense conversations can signal a healthy team. But there still needs to be someone in the room with enough power to keep the conversation on track, on time, and thoroughly professional.

Sign #3 That You're Too Soft: You Regularly Mediate Other People's Conflicts

It's troubling when a leader is regularly sucked into employee conflicts. In an ideal world, employees would act like adults and resolve conflicts themselves using Truth Talks, reserving the boss-as-mediator for only the most serious issues. But when a leader has become too accommodating, employees quickly figure out that if they plead their case, the boss will intervene on their behalf. It's quite similar to the games that kids play—whether it's "Ma, he's looking at me funny" or playing one parent off another.

When a leader has a reputation as being focused on facts, these manipulations are rare. But when the leader is seen as overly accommodating or appeasing, these games will be a frequent occurrence.

Sign #4 That You're Too Soft: You See the Same Problem Multiple Times

There isn't an organization on the planet that doesn't have people who make mistakes. That's the price of doing business. But when you see people making the same mistakes again and again, it's often a sign that they haven't heard the truth that they need to improve. And that's often the result of employees believing that their gentle leader won't really follow through on enforcing consequences.

I'm not suggesting that we should all move to the opposite extreme, where people are risk-averse and paralyzed by fear of being fired. That's every bit as damaging. Rather, an organization built on truth will find the middle ground where mistakes may be inevitable, but we all strive to avoid making the same mistake repeatedly.

These four signs will alert you to potential problems with excessive softness and insufficient truthfulness. But what are the communication practices that cause this excessive softness? The Compliment Sandwich, Shirking, and Advice are the three that I've found contribute the most to this softness problem. Let's take a look at each of them.

Communication Error #1: The Compliment Sandwich

Truth Talks maintain a delicate balance. When our words are too harsh, our truth partners shut down emotionally, get defensive, and fail to hear a word we say. But when we soft-pedal the truth, our truth partners fail to hear the message that they really do need to change.

It's a difficult balance to maintain, and among leaders only a minority strike it effectively. Lately, there's a real trend toward excessive softness. I recently conducted a three-question quiz (you can take the quiz for yourself at http://www.leadershipiq.com/blogs/leadershipiq/39841409-quiz-whats-your-communication-style) that assessed how over 1,800 leaders deliver constructive criticism. One of the questions asked respondents to indicate which statement best represented them, and here are the four possible choices:

1. Employees need to know the cut-and-dried facts about whether their performance was bad, good, or great. But I don't get into emotional discussions of my feelings about their performance.
2. I don't have time to give constant feedback. If my employees want to know about the quality of their performance, they can schedule time to talk to me.
3. Of course some employees feel criticized or offended by my words. Constructive criticism is supposed to be tough. It's constructive, but it's still criticism.
4. I make constructive criticism easier to hear. I often use a compliment sandwich (a nice compliment, followed by a bit of criticism, followed by another nice compliment). If the employee shuts me out, he or she won't improve.

About 31 percent of respondents chose answer number one, which is good because that's the answer associated with the most effective constructive criticism. Only 3 percent chose answer number two (a laissez-faire approach), and 14 percent chose answer number three (a harsh approach). What concerns me is that 51 percent of respondents chose answer number four.[1] Now, some of the sentiment in that answer is fine; you don't want employees to shut you out. But the compliment sandwich is rarely, if ever, a good approach to delivering constructive criticism.

Imagine your boss calls you in to deliver some constructive criticism in the form of a compliment sandwich. You might hear the boss say this: "You're a world-class talent, the absolute best. You're probably the smartest person in the department. Now, you've been pretty nasty during our weekly meetings, and it's causing some hurt feelings. But I'm saying all this because you're just so darn talented and I want to see you shine."

All I hear in that message is that I'm really smart and talented. I just wrote the boss's words, and it's honestly hard for me to remember the criticism in the middle without rereading it. The constructive criticism is incongruous with all the compliments, and as a practical matter, people don't usually remember the stuff that comes in the middle. This is what psychology calls the serial position effect. If, for example, you were asked to remember a list of words, you'd likely remember the words at the beginning of the list and the words at the end of the list. And you'd probably forget the ones in the middle.

It's worth noting that, depending on the study, the recall for the words at the end can be three to five times higher than for the words in the middle! (If that doesn't make the case for not sandwiching your constructive criticism, I'm not sure what will.) I'm not suggesting that you should call employees into your office and verbally bludgeon them. As I've noted throughout this book, that's equally ineffective. But we have an obligation to help our employees improve. And it's abdicating our responsibilities to sugarcoat and water down our messages to the point where people don't understand that they need to improve.

Communication Error #2: Shirking

To be a great leader, you can't fear being seen as the bad guy or gal. And I'm not just talking about obvious "bad guy/gal" situations like telling someone "You're fired" or "You're not getting a raise this year, and here's why." Being seen as the bad guy/gal also includes situations like telling someone, "I need you to change the way you submit that form." Great leaders give constructive criticism and other tough feedback. And when you do, you've got to own it, even if that means being seen as the bad guy/gal.

Shirking is the opposite of owning your feedback. It's basically saying to someone, "Listen, I think you're doing a great job. But Bob, the new VP, he's not so happy with some of your work, and we're going to have to talk about that." Shirking is giving tough feedback but ascribing it to someone else. It's done to try to slip out of being the bad guy/gal, and not surprisingly, shirking usually backfires.

Shirking shows up all over the place. You hear it in situations like these:

- "You know I'd give you an 8 percent raise if I could, but the new VP is staying firm on 2 percent."
- "You know I don't have a problem keeping you on the account, but the CEO must have overheard something you said to the client. The CEO made the call on this one. I don't really have any control."
- "We're pulling back on remote work hours. I think it's been working out fine, but the HR team wants folks back in the office."

Ascribing our feedback to someone else is an abdication of our responsibility as leaders. And shirking (*a*) ruins employee relationship building, (*b*) destroys leadership camaraderie, and (*c*) encourages a culture of blame in the organization.

Having the guts to give your folks tough news doesn't make you the enemy. It makes you a leader who helps your people to grow and to develop and to achieve great things. When you shirk the responsibility for that news onto someone else, the lesson gets lost. The only thing the employee learns is, "Wow, that new VP is a real jerk." And that can unleash a whole new set of behavioral problems as the employee now sees the new VP as the enemy instead of the exciting new leader who is going to turn the company around.

Leave the new VP (or CEO or HR team) out of it and approach the feedback with fact-based communication that tells your people "Awesome performance looks like this: _____, and your performance doesn't look like that, so let's talk about how to get you to awesome." Owning feedback in this way, instead of blaming someone else, carries weight. It lets your people know you're serious, it engenders respect, and it makes people accountable to making the desired behavioral changes. It's the foundation on which employee-manager relationships are built.

Another reason Shirking is unadvisable is that it puts you in the hot seat with whomever you threw under bus. The peers and bosses you point the finger at won't appreciate playing your scapegoat, even if the tough feedback did originate with them. Let's say Pat, the new VP, really did walk into your office. And Pat really did say, "Your guy is screwing up communication with the client, and I want him off the project." Telling your employee the feedback comes from Pat won't win you any points. The odds are pretty good that Pat came to you with this information for a reason, namely an invitation to do your job. Shirking positions you as someone who can't do the job, who blames, or who stirs up organizational drama. Your peers and bosses will lose trust in you and stop sharing the valuable critical feedback that you need to do your job well.

Finally, if we throw Pat, or the new CEO, or anyone else under the bus, we have basically said to our employees, "It's okay in this organization to throw people under the bus. Look at how I just did it! So go ahead and blame. Forget all that stuff we've been spoon-feeding you about being accountable. In this workplace, blame is the game!" The research on this is clear: blame is contagious. The more we blame others, the more the people around us are going to feel it's okay for them to blame others as well.

Bottom line, if you have critical feedback to give, you've got to own that feedback. Don't throw your colleagues or bosses under the bus by shirking. Stick to fact-based conversations. It will bolster your bravery by allowing you to speak candidly without making people angry so you can turn tough conversations into coaching conversations that result in positive behavioral change.

Communication Error #3: Advice

Do you give advice? At one time or another we all do, but did you know people really hate getting advice? They rarely take advice, and in fact, folks often get defensive, angry, or insulted when it's offered. And just so we're clear, any statement that contains words like *should*, *would*, *ought*, *got to*, *must*, and *try* is advice. For example:

- "I wouldn't say that to him."
- "If it were me, I'd wear the blue tie."
- "Have you tried rebooting it?"

- "You should talk to Bob; he really knows what he's doing."
- "You've got to try the other market; the prices are much better."

Here are the top five reasons why giving advice doesn't work.

Why Advice Doesn't Work Reason #1: Judgment

When you give somebody unsolicited advice, it sends an underlying and very judgmental message of "You're obviously not as savvy as I am, because if you were, you'd have already figured out what I'm telling you." You may not consciously intend to promote this message, but it's what the person on the receiving end of your advice is likely hearing.

What's more, if you continually offer unsolicited advice, there's a good chance folks will retaliate by letting you know, in no uncertain terms, about your own faults. You may think you're being helpful, or you may truly think you know better, but you're not going to convince anyone who's stuck listening to you. Anyone on the other end of your endless stream of "You should . . . you'd better . . ." is probably thinking, "Who the heck is this bozo to be giving me advice? He should clean up his own mess and then come talk to me."

Why Advice Doesn't Work Reason #2: Directive

When you give unsolicited advice, in essence, you're telling somebody else what to do. This implies you have all the answers about what will and won't work. But how could you? Chances are you don't have all the background information on the situation, nor do you understand the other person's emotions and what makes him or her tick. This makes you anything but an expert.

There's absolutely no constructive value in statements like "Well, if it were me, I would _____." It's not you, and it's not up to you to decide what to do. Providing unsolicited advice only puts your truth partner on red alert as he or she checks out of the conversation to build up the Walls of Defensiveness. Asking questions that provide additional facts about the situation is far more productive. But be careful. Sometimes the questions we ask are no more than a thinly disguised form of unsolicited advice.

I had a recent experience where my laptop froze while I was at a client site. The client called in his tech support department, and the first thing one of the IT guys asked me was, "Did you try rebooting it?" Now, that may be the question everybody asks, but it's not a question; it's really a directive, and that means it's advice. Here's the internal reaction I had to his "advice question":

I thought sarcastically, "Holy mackerel, you mean you can restart a laptop? Why didn't I think of that? I mean, every day I turn it *on*, but I never thought about turning it *off*. They clearly don't pay you enough because that is absolute *genius*!"

Of course, I bit my tongue and answered his question. But what if he'd instead asked me, "What actions have you taken so far?" There's a big difference between that and "Did you try rebooting it?" One is a legitimate attempt to gather information, while the other is unsolicited advice.

I don't mean to imply that you should never be directive. When you're a superior telling a subordinate what to do, it's perfectly acceptable. But even in that situation, you still need to be careful that you're giving directions, not advice. Because if you give advice, you're only setting the stage for a terrible dynamic. Here's an example of what I mean in a scenario where a boss sees her employee writing a report:

Boss: "I wouldn't use those colors for that report. I'd go with something brighter."
Employee: "Sure, okay."

Fast-forward to later that day, when the employee has finished the report and presented it to the boss:

Boss: "What the heck is this? I told you to use brighter colors."
Employee: "No, you said *you* would use something brighter. I liked the colors I was already using just fine."
Boss: "Listen, when I tell you to do something, I just want you to do it."
Employee: "Then next time tell me what you want."

As a superior you have the right (and obligation) to give directions and make corrections. However, when you phrase it as advice, it sounds more like a recommendation than a directive. And as we've seen, that creates a misunderstanding that wastes everyone's time.

To avoid these kinds of situations, follow this simple rule: If what you need to tell subordinates is not optional, then be honest with them. Don't play coy and pretend they have a choice when actually they don't.

Why Advice Doesn't Work Reason #3: Inflexibility

When you give advice, you offer your listener only two choices: take the advice or ignore the advice. If your advice is taken, that means your listener must tacitly admit you're right and he or she is wrong. This automatically gives you credit for being smarter. This is a dangerous scenario, and it's one that's almost guaranteed to send your truth partner's Walls of Defensiveness skyward.

When advice is ignored, it invites the possibility of an" I told you so," thus prompting yet more defensiveness. Even if you outwardly don't acknowledge the failure to take your advice, the person who passed on taking it may fear you're insulted. This scenario can shut someone down from attempting any future discussion on the topic (or any other topic for that matter). And then there's always the chance that your constant advice and inflexibility has you positioned as someone to be avoided.

Why Advice Doesn't Work Reason #4: Narcissism

Let's be honest. Sometimes we give advice to demonstrate how smart we are, or because we feel left out or need to be needed. But we do it under the guise of trying to be helpful.

Leesa started with a top PR firm right out of college. Over the years she worked her way up to account director. Despite her professional success, she's hindered by childhood insecurities of not being good enough. To counter this, Leesa has a history of imparting unasked-for advice to any coworker that will listen. When someone takes her advice and succeeds, Leesa is right there to take all the credit. But eventually her coworkers caught on, and now they make sure to shut her down before she opens her mouth.

Truth Talks are about being heard and getting results, not about personal kudos and pats on the back. If your focus is on getting all the credit when success is achieved, you leave your truth partner no choice but to admit you're smarter, better, wiser, and stronger. This is a surefire way to foment Psychological Resistance.

Why Advice Doesn't Work Reason #5: Unsolicited

Most advice is offered unsolicited. This means the other party didn't ask to be judged, corrected, or directed—he or she was just making everyday chitchat. When you catch people off guard and hit them upside the head with advice, there's virtually no chance they'll be in an open emotional state to hear what you say.

What if someone asks you for advice? True story: The other morning I walked downstairs fully dressed and wearing a new shirt and tie, and I asked my wife, Andrea, "Do you think I should wear this red tie with this shirt?"

Now seriously, what answer do you think I was looking for? Was I hoping she would tell me I shouldn't be allowed to dress myself because my color choices are so horrible? Did I really want to walk all the way back upstairs and change? Of course not; I wanted an affirmation that I looked good, and that's it.

Although you can find incredibly rare exceptions (and I mean really rare), nobody who has ever asked for advice really wanted it. The reason is people are already committed to a course of action. If you give contrary advice, they've got to undo everything and start all over. If somebody truly wanted input, he'd have asked for it before he got started (like before I put on my tie). But that's not typically how the world works.

Imagine if Andrea had given me advice and said, "I personally would never match those colors."

If I allowed her advice to raise my resistance, my reply would likely be along the lines of, "Well, that's because you don't know about fashion."

In return, she might retaliate with something like, "Well if I don't know about fashion, then why'd you ask me?" And on it would go until I found myself in a heap of trouble: all because I wanted to hear that I looked good. You can see how easily things can go wrong when you give advice.

Another reason some folks ask for advice is as a lead-in to a fight. In one case, Gladys had been jealous of and competitive with her older sister since they were kids. She was always on the lookout for ways to put Risa down. When the company Risa worked for downsized and fired her, Gladys called her sister, professedly to console her. Gladys purposely slipped in how unhappy she was with her own career, saying, "I just don't know what to do," and then she waited, hoping Risa would take the bait.

When Risa suggested she might want to look elsewhere, even offering some of her job contacts, Gladys immediately lashed back with, "As if you're one to be giving advice! At least I can hold on to a job." After a while Risa caught on to Gladys's ploy to start trouble, but not before some major battles took place.

You might not want to admit to it, but nearly all of us have asked someone for advice in the hope that the person would give the "wrong answer" and open the door for us to feel superior and/or air a lot of grievances. This may provide a dumping ground for a lot of discontent, but it's not speaking the truth.

THE TOUGHNESS PROBLEM

On the opposite end of the spectrum from the softness problem lies the toughness problem. Sometimes we can push people so hard that performance suffers. I get it: there's huge pressure on all of us to achieve results. But there's a fine line between pushing people to achieve greatness and pushing so hard that people crack. Here are three signs that the facts you are sharing are too tough.

Sign #1 That You're Too Tough: You Walk into a Room and People Stop Talking

One of the surest signs that you've crossed the line from respect to fear is when you walk into a room and the chatter immediately turns to silence. Contrary to popular belief, this does not mean people were talking about you. But it's often a sign that they are afraid of you.

Remember back in high school when you had that really tough teacher, who as soon as she entered the classroom all the students "zipped it" for fear of getting yelled at (or sent to the principal's office)? If you enter a room and have flashbacks to that tough teacher, you may have strayed from respected to feared.

We all like meetings to quickly come to order. And it's perfectly normal to not want your office to be a coffee klatch. But there's a difference between a room that quiets gently when you enter versus people shutting up midsentence out of fear.

Sign #2 That You're Too Tough: When You Give Constructive Feedback, Employees Are Very Quiet

Every leader (regardless of his or her leadership style) is going to give tough feedback or constructive criticism. But ideally, when you give that feedback, the recipients will have a response or ask questions. Maybe they ask for clarification. Or perhaps they share their side of things. Occasionally they might respectfully disagree. And in a perfect world, they'll say something like "Gee, you're right . . . I totally get it now and I'll make a change."

But when the recipient of your constructive criticism sits there quietly, without much response, it's often an indicator of having gone into mental shutdown (perhaps to survive the verbal beating). When constructive feedback is delivered too harshly, the recipient can get defensive, shut down mentally, and never make a corrective leap. He or she fails to do anything positive or productive with the feedback. If you observe this response happening often, especially if it's with more than one of your employees, you may need to dial down on the toughness and focus on delivering more "constructive" and less "criticism."

Sign #3 That You're Too Tough: You Do More Than 60 Percent of the Talking in Meetings

Occasionally when I'm coaching senior executives, I'll attend a few of their meetings. One of the metrics I track is how many minutes the executive talks versus everyone else in the room (I literally use a stopwatch just like an old-school gym teacher). If the executive does more than 60 percent of the talking, it's a pretty good sign that his or her leadership style has gotten too tough.

There's a difference between a meeting and an assembly. In an assembly, it's perfectly legitimate to call people into the room and deliver a soliloquy with a bunch of information. If you've got a big announcement or a new policy change, the largely one-way flow of information can be acceptable.

But meetings are different. In a meeting, you brought those people into the room to solicit and gather their input, to elicit their great ideas, and to avail yourself of their innovative thoughts. That won't happen if you're doing all of the talking.

Sometimes leaders do all the talking because they have trouble sitting quietly (whether from ego or ADHD or whatever). But sometimes leaders do all the talking because their employees are too afraid to open their mouths. This situation can cause a lot of trouble. Test this out in your next meeting. Stop talking for a few minutes. If your employees naturally pick up the conversation, you're probably okay. But if there's an awkward lull, or people just stare, waiting for you to speak again, there's an issue.

Those three signs will alert you to potential problems with excessive toughness and aggressive truthfulness. But what are the communication practices that cause this excessive toughness? Blaming and Cocksureness are the two practices that I've found contribute most to this toughness problem. Let's take a look at them both.

Communication Error #1: Blaming

Blame is often confused with holding someone responsible. When you hold someone responsible for a mistake, you're essentially saying, "This issue is your responsibility. It went wrong, and regardless of why that happened, you're responsible for fixing it." The person on the receiving end of your words may not feel great about the situation, but it's likely he or she will absorb what you said and fix the problem.

In contrast to this, when you blame someone for a mistake, it typically comes off sounding something like this: "This issue is your responsibility. It went wrong, it's all your fault, and you should feel ashamed, embarrassed, and worthless for having let it happen." Blame is an emotional attack, and as soon as it's launched, it increases resistance.

Holding someone responsible is about assigning a repair job, not fault. While assigning responsibility generally concerns bad news, it tends to be forward-looking and constructive. Who cares who caused the mistake as long as we know who will fix it? And even if we do know who caused the mistake, fixing the blunder is still our top priority.

Blame is almost never constructive. Its destructive power stems largely from its negative emotional content. Blamers are far more concerned with making the blamed feel awful than they are with getting the problem fixed.

Jilly found herself in the unwelcome position of having to tell her boss that a major client was taking his business to a main competitor. She had done everything she could to try to retain the client, but her company just didn't have the equipment or manpower to fulfill his orders while the other company did.

She knew her boss would take the news badly, but she didn't expect to be blamed for the situation. So she was greatly surprised when the boss said, "Why didn't you bring this to me sooner? If you had told me earlier, I could have fixed this and undone your screwup!" Jilly took the abuse silently and went back to her desk, but she made sure all her coworkers knew about their boss's irrational outburst. In the end, the client was lost and the whole workplace thought the boss was a jerk. How much better it would have been if the boss had said, "Let's not worry about whose fault it is. Right now, let's focus on winning back the client."

Because it's historical and emotional, there's no real benefit to blame. Can you think of one time when you made someone else feel bad and it helped to solve a problem? And even if there is some short-term emotional boost from unloading on people and making sure they know they messed up, ask yourself this: "If I make this person feel awful, do I increase or decrease the effectiveness of having him or her help fix the problem?"

"You" and "We" Statements

How many times have you heard someone say, "You're not making any sense"? Think back on your own experiences of when those words were spoken to you. Did you smile and say, "Gee, I'm sorry. Let me try again"? Probably not, and if you did, it was likely because you felt forced to do so. There's a better chance you mentally checked out of the conversation or verbally struck back in anger.

While "You're not making any sense" may sound innocuous enough at first, it points the "you" finger of blame. It implies the other person lacks knowledge and understanding, and expresses a belief that he or she is incapable of presenting a clear argument. Bottom line, when you say "you," it sounds aggressive and attacking.

Just as bad as "you" is using the word *we* when what you really mean is "you." Here's an example that shows what I mean. Charles owns his own marketing company, and his wife, Mirabelle, takes care of the bookkeeping. Charles is a big believer in spending money to make money. He advertises big, has a lot of employees, and does a lot of client entertaining.

Mirabelle is cautious with money and views Charles's spending as extravagant and unnecessary. She regularly makes her feelings known with statements like, "I've been looking over the books, and we really need to be more conservative with our spending" and "Don't you think we should eat at home more often?"

It's obvious to Charles that Mirabelle blames him for spending the money he works hard to earn. Most times he flippantly responds to her blame statements with something like, "Absolutely. I think you should definitely be more careful with our money." Mirabelle continues to get frustrated, and Charles continues to spend.

"You're Not Listening to Me" and "Listen to Me"

Blame can also be found in these two statements: "You're not listening to me" and it's shorter cousin, "Listen to me." Both these statements convey the sentiment that "My message is perfect and any lack of understanding can be attributed to your lack of attention." Or they could also imply, "Once you do pay attention, you will undoubtedly agree with me; and if you don't, there must be something wrong with you." Either way, these statements are filled with recrimination and are guaranteed to increase your truth partner's Psychological Resistance.

Imagine we didn't blame the other person. Suppose that instead we take full responsibility for the lack of understanding. After all, does it really matter why somebody isn't getting our message? Isn't the more important issue getting that person to understand our message?

As a starting point, we could rewrite the statement "You're not making any sense" into "Could you help me understand this issue?" Just as we could rewrite "You're not listening to me" as "I don't think I'm doing a good job of explaining myself."

Anybody would feel a lot less defensive being on the receiving end of the rewritten statements. The rewrites don't cast blame; instead they state that the speaker takes full responsibility for any lack of shared understanding. What's more, these simple rewrites extend a hand of collaboration and ask for our truth partner's assistance in achieving understanding.

Communication Error #2: Cocksureness

Cocksureness is when you're so certain about your position, so inappropriately conceited, that you're guaranteed to make the Walls of Defensiveness rise. Cocksureness can be heard in commonly uttered statements such as the following:

- "Whoever votes for [insert name] is a moron."
- "[Insert country or city] is an unfixable mess."
- "Pink Floyd sucks."
- "Pink Floyd invented psychedelic rock and made modern-day alternative music possible. All these copycats today should be sending them royalty checks because they wouldn't even exist without Pink Floyd."

Cocksure statements send out a loud message that proclaims: "Don't even bother discussing this with me. I know what I know, and you're not going to penetrate my consciousness and convince me otherwise."

There are two significant problems with Cocksureness. The first is that it signals to any potential conversation partner that there's only one possible outcome of this conversation: agree with me.

The second problem is that it implies everyone else is an idiot. It says, "I have some special insight into this issue. Obviously, you don't have that insight, or I wouldn't have to tell you about it. And if you still don't agree with my special insight after I've shared it, then you really must be dumb."

Ultimately, Truth Talks are adult-to-adult conversations that share just enough facts to help our truth partners make a corrective leap. Once their light bulb is on, it's time to move forward by saying, "Let's talk about how we can make things better in the future." If the conversation isn't focused on making change, it isn't a Truth Talk.

If you hear blame instead of a corrective leap, redirect the conversation back to the central issue with the simple statement, "Let's discuss what we *can* control."

Truth Talks require a delicate balance. The Compliment Sandwich, Shirking, and Advice are faulty communication practices that will turn your Truth Talk soft and ineffective. Look for warning signs including conversations that go on too long or get off topic, getting sucked into mediating other people's conflicts, and seeing the same mistakes repeated multiple times.

Conversely, excessive toughness and aggressive truthfulness will send your truth partner into mental shutdown and derail a Truth Talk. Look for signs that you've crossed the line including encountering a sudden silence when you enter a room, experiencing a lack of response to your feedback, and doing more than 60 percent of the talking. Blaming and Cocksureness are the two communication practices that contribute most to the toughness problem.

CONCLUSION

We've covered a lot in this book. So as we conclude, let's take a brisk walk back through the essentials of conducting a Truth Talk.

THE EIGHT STEPS TO A TRUTH TALK

The eight steps to a Truth Talk are as follows:

- **Step 1:** Understand the Truth-Killers (or Why We Resist the Truth)
- **Step 2:** Focus on the Facts
- **Step 3:** Take Their Perspective
- **Step 4:** Set Your Goals
- **Step 5:** Start a Conversation, Not a Confrontation
- **Step 6:** Create a Word Picture
- **Step 7:** Listen with Structure
- **Step 8:** Share the Facts

Let's review some of the key points for each of these steps.

Step 1: Understand the Truth-Killers (or Why We Resist the Truth)

As you enter a Truth Talk, look for signs of Confident Unawareness, Perceptual Resistance, Psychological Resistance, and Financial Resistance. These four Truth-Killers are the biggest reasons why people fail to recognize and accept the truth.

Confident Unawareness (not knowing what you are sure you do know) occurs due to poor training, a lack of feedback, or the Dunning-Kruger effect, a cognitive bias whereby people who are incompetent at something are unable to recognize their own incompetence.

It's not easy to tell people your truth when they experience a completely different truth. The Truth-Killer of **Perceptual Resistance** is influenced by differing worldviews and preexisting frames of reference. Your truth partner won't be receptive to your feedback, but he or she is not unaware that you might see things differently.

Psychological Resistance is a response to the discomfort felt from simultaneously holding two opposing beliefs. When this cognitive dissonance occurs, the tendency is to ease the tension by going with whichever belief works best for the ego.

Finally, money talks, even in Truth Talks, and the incentive of financial reward causes our fourth Truth-Killer, **Financial Resistance**.

Step 2: Focus on the Facts

Before you can start a Truth Talk, you've got to understand what the truth really is. Every conversation has four layers: **Facts**, **Interpretations**, **Reactions**, and **Ends** (the **FIRE Model**). The best way to ensure that your truth partner listens to your message is to drop all the **I**nterpretations, **R**eactions, and **E**nds (**IRE**, the emotional baggage, judgment, and negative energy) and just focus on the Facts.

SCOUT for the facts to separate them from the IRE. Make sure the facts are **S**pecific, **C**andid, **O**bjective, **U**nemotional, and **T**imely. Here are a few tips to remember about facts:

- Facts should be clear and should never include words like *always*, *never*, *forever*, *impossible*, and *constantly*.
- Timely facts lead to more productive and less emotional conversations.
- Facts are candid, so don't soft-pedal the truth. We often tell ourselves that softening our message is for the good of the recipient. But we're really doing it to spare ourselves the anticipated discomfort of sharing candid facts.

Thinking factually also reduces our emotional baggage. We've all had conversations in which we struggled to focus on the present situation due to the distraction of past baggage swirling around in our heads. The FIRE Model acts as a mental filter for reevaluating these situations.

Step 3: Take Their Perspective

Once you've distilled the facts, it's time to climb inside your truth partner's mind and see the situation from his or her perspective. **Perspective-taking** is a powerful way to get people plugged in and listening when you have a tough message to share.

When our truth partner sees that we're trying to see the world, or a particular situation, from his or her viewpoint, it helps make that person feel heard and understood. It signals that we're not coming to attack or insult. In response, our truth partner's defensiveness drops and he or she becomes more open-minded to what we have to say.

Make perspective-taking easier by using the four Truth-Killers as a mental checklist. Assess whether your truth partner is experiencing Confident Unawareness, Psychological Resistance, Perceptual Resistance, or Financial Resistance. When you see your truth partner as a unique individual, it's a lot easier to take his or her perspective than when you see the person as an anonymous member of a group. Facilitate this by saying your truth partner's name, in your head or out loud. Put it into a sentence like "I'm going to have a Truth Talk with Jane/Bob/etc."

Step 4: Set Your Goals

Once you've clarified your facts and you understand your truth partner's perspective, it's time to assess what you can realistically achieve in your Truth Talk. If the facts are especially difficult and your truth partner is experiencing several Truth-Killers, you may need to take a more staged approach to your Truth Talk. But before you set an effective goal for your Truth Talk, be sure you aren't setting one of these three bad goals:

Bad Goal #1: I Want an Apology

Wanting someone to say "I'm sorry" is a popular goal when hard truths are at stake. But if you try and force an apology, there's no guarantee that what you'll get is a sincere apology that inspires permanent behavioral change. Remember, helping your truth partner to change something that is destructive is the reason you're having this Truth Talk.

Bad Goal #2: I Want You to Admit You Were Wrong

It's a common belief that getting someone to admit a wrongdoing is a great way to get that person to see that you are right. But it doesn't work. Bringing a combative winner-loser mentality of "I want you to admit you were wrong and that I'm right" to a Truth Talk will turn the conversation toxic.

Bad Goal #3: I Want You to Feel Bad for What You Did

Setting a goal to get someone to feel bad is never a good idea. A Truth Talk isn't about blowing off steam or exacting revenge. Creating positive change requires a goal that is both rational and strategic

The 6 Months Later Technique

The 6 Months Later Technique helps take you outside the emotional distraction so you can view your goal objectively. Start by picturing yourself and your truth partner interacting six months from now. While envisioning this future interaction, answer these four questions:

1. In six months, what do I want our relationship to be like?
2. In six months, what changes do I want to have occurred?
3. In six months, what do I want to be doing?
4. In six months, what do I want my truth partner to be doing?

The answers to these four questions form your goal.

Once we've used the 6 Months Later Technique to create a goal for our Truth Talk, there is one more consideration: strategy. Some goals can be handled in a 15-minute conversation, while others may take an hour. And then there will be conversations that require multiple separate conversations. Two factors that can help determine strategy, such as whether you're headed into a one-time talk or multiple-conversation process, are (1) the complexity of your goals and (2) the intensity of the resistance you'll face. Here are the four possible combinations you might face:

1. Simple goals and little resistance (requires a single, brief Truth Talk)
2. Complex goals and little resistance (requires a single but longer Truth Talk)
3. Simple goals and deep resistance (requires a longer and more intense Truth Talk)
4. Complex goals and deep resistance (requires a multistage Truth Talk)

Step 5: Start a Conversation, Not a Confrontation

Have you ever tried to have a conversation with someone about something important, but that person just wouldn't listen? The frustration is enough to make you want to grab the person and shake your words into his brain. But confrontations don't work.

Confrontation only invites resistance, like refusing to make eye contact, remaining silent, offering monosyllabic responses, claiming lack of memory, discussing an unrelated topic, providing well-known information, providing a scripted response, retracting previous statements, andgiving "no-comment" answers.

The only surefire way to initiate change is to send a message that awakens a commitment from your truth partner using a five-part process called the IDEAS script. This simple script provides an opening that establishes a dialogue (not a diatribe) and signals to your truth partner that you "come in peace" to learn and share, not fight and yell. The IDEAS script doesn't soften your message, but by following the script, you communicate that you're going to discuss the issues, not shout about them.

The Five Steps of the IDEAS Script

- **Step 1. I:** Invite them to partner. "Would you be willing to have a conversation with me about XYZ?"
- **Step 2. D:** Disarm yourself. "I'd like to review the situation to make sure I'm on the same page as you."
- **Step 3. E:** Eliminate blame. "And if we have different perspectives, we can discuss those and develop a plan for moving forward."
- **Step 4. A:** Affirm their control. "Does that sound okay to you?"
- **Step 5. S:** Set a time limit. "Do you want to talk now, or would you prefer to wait until after lunch?"

Each step in the IDEAS script has a distinct purpose. When applied collectively, the steps generate a domino effect that drastically reduces your listener's resistance, making him or her a true partner in conversation.

The Power of Questions

A theme throughout this book is the power of asking questions, sometimes even numerous times. Notice how there's a pretty even split between asking questions and making statements in the IDEAS script? That's by design. The purpose of the IDEAS script is to turn a potential confrontation into a conversation, and the only way we're going to make that transformation is by drawing the other person out with questions.

When you ask questions, like in the IDEAS script, there's always the risk that the other person will say "No! I don't want to have a conversation with you." It's a lot less common than we imagine, but it does happen on occasion. Don't be afraid of hearing no. It's okay, because when people say no, they're telling us that they're worried about where the conversation is headed. When someone says no, respond with another question, such as, "May I ask why?" The goal is to discover the source of your truth partner's resistance, and when we respond with thoughtfulness and curiosity, we're further demonstrating our commitment to understanding the person's perspective.

Step 6: Create a Word Picture

When everyone has a different definition of the truth, an argument is virtually guaranteed. And far too many disagreements occur because we don't have a clear and shared definition of the truth. So we're going to create a Word Picture: a tripartite definition that transforms abstract concepts into concrete examples that anyone can understand.

By using a tripartite definition (bad, good, and great), and providing concrete examples of each, we're borrowing from an instructional approach called Concept Attainment. Concept Attainment involves learning an abstract concept through studying examples and nonexamples.

In the world of tough conversations, it's a good idea to create examples, nonexamples, and super-examples. People understand abstract concepts faster and better with examples that teach how to do something well, how not to do something, and how to do that something incredibly well.

It's also beneficial to use concrete words, phrases, and sentences, as they are found to be more comprehensible, memorable, and interesting than abstract language.

The goal here is to generate some cognitive dissonance by having people compare the idealized Word Picture with their real-life performance.

Step 7: Listen with Structure

One of the critical skills you'll need to conduct a Truth Talk has nothing to do with talking; rather, it's all about listening. Once you've set your goals, begun a dialogue, and created a Word Picture, you're going to hit a point in the conversation where your truth partner will really start talking. People will share what's going on inside their head, reveal their interpretations, reactions, and ends, and basically tell you everything you should know to engage them effectively. If you don't listen deeply, you'll never get any of that information. And without listening, you won't have a Truth Talk; you'll just have a reciprocated diatribe.

There are seven commonly uttered phrases that clearly say, "I'm not listening." You may not always hear the exact version listed below, but you've certainly heard some variation.

- **Phrase #1:** "Griping about it won't make it better."
- **Phrase #2:** "Suck it up."
- **Phrase #3:** "Life is unfair."
- **Phrase #4:** "Maybe it's a blessing in disguise."
- **Phrase #5:** "Don't worry; you'll get over it."
- **Phrase #6:** "You think you've got problems?"
- **Phrase #7:** "Yes, but."

In addition to avoiding these seven phrases, don't interrupt your truth partner. Interrupting seriously hampers communication, ruins our reputation as "someone people can talk to," and typically infuriates the person who gets interrupted.

Structured Listening

Listening effectively requires a process that positively impacts the person speaking, gets us the appropriate information, and fully engages our brain. The process we're going to employ, Structured Listening, involves three parts: eliciting, listening, and confirming.

1. **Eliciting.** Eliciting is where we communicate to our truth partner that we want to hear his or her thoughts and encourage the person to share those thoughts.
2. **Listening.** Listening involves keeping our lips sealed, ears open, and brain active. Using the FIRE Model will help bring structure to the conversation.
3. **Confirming.** Confirming is when we corroborate that we understood our truth partner correctly.

Step 8: Share the Facts

When we're ready to share the facts, we're going to share just enough to ensure that our truth partner makes a corrective leap. We need our truth partner to make a corrective leap because once the person's light bulb is on, we can then say, "Let's talk about how we can make things better in the future."

This is the time in a Truth Talk when we can brainstorm, problem-solve, and otherwise plot a positive future. Far too many difficult conversations get stuck in looking backward, discussing ad nauseam all the things that went wrong. While we do need to look backward a bit to create a corrective leap, ideally we're going to spend the bulk of our time designing a better future.

Blame

Blame is aggressive and attacking and very unhealthy. Blame is highly contagious, and when people blame each other, it's up to us to turn that blame into accountability by using six simple words: "Let's discuss what we *can* control."

The Softness Problem

One of the mistakes people make when sharing the facts is being too soft, which obfuscates the truth. There's significant pressure in today's organizations for everyone to be engaged, be inspired, have fun, and be fulfilled. And that's a great thing. But one of the potential unintended consequences of that pressure is that our conversations become focused on making people happy instead of making them more effective. So we need to avoid the three practices that contribute most to this softness problem: the Compliment Sandwich, Shirking, and Advice.

The Toughness Problem

On the opposite end of the spectrum lies the toughness problem. There's a fine line between pushing people to achieve greatness and pushing so hard that people crack. So we need to avoid the two practices that I've found contribute most to this toughness problem: Blaming and Cocksureness.

WRAP-UP

So there you have it. A Truth Talk is a conversational process in which you can speak hard truths and your truth partner will accept and embrace those truths. More technically, a Truth Talk is a fact-based dialogic process that reduces the listener's psychological barriers to hearing, accepting, and acting upon hard truths. Whether you're trying to gain acceptance for a brilliant discovery, convince an employee to get to work on time, stop your coworker from being a jerk, or urge your boss to tell you the truth about why she's mad, a Truth Talk makes hard truths easy to hear.

NOTES

INTRODUCTION

1. K. Codell Carter and Barbara R. Carter, *Childbed Fever: A Scientific Biography of Ignaz Semmelweis* (Westport, CT: Greenwood, 1994).

2. Gretchen Gavett, "Can GM Make It Safe for Employees to Speak Up?," *Harvard Business Review*, June 5, 2014.

3. Richard M. J. Bohmer, Amy C. Edmondson, Michael Roberto, Laura Feldman, and Erika Ferlins, "Columbia's Final Mission," Harvard Business School Multimedia/Video Case 305-032, March 2005. (Revised May 2009.)

4. Rodger Dean Duncan, "Is There an Elephant in the Room? Name It and Tame It," *Forbes*, October 14, 2014, accessed October 2, 2016, https://www.forbes.com/sites/rodgerdeanduncan/2014/10/14/is-there-an-elephant-in-the-room-name-it-and-tame-it/.

5. "Employee Engagement Shocker: Low Performers May Be MORE Engaged Than High Performers," *The Blog* by Mark Murphy and Leadership IQ, http://www.leadershipiq.com/blogs/leadershipiq/35354881-employee-engagement-shocker-low-performers-may-be-more-engaged-than-high-performers.

6. Lauren Weber, "Bad at Their Jobs, and Loving It," *Wall Street Journal* (web log), May 27, 2013, http://blogs.wsj.com/atwork/2013/03/27/bad-at-their-jobs-and-loving-it/?mod=WSJ_Management_At_Work.

7. Barry J. Marshall, *Helicobacter Pioneers: Firsthand Accounts from the Scientists Who Discovered Helicobacters, 1892–1982* (Victoria, Australia: Blackwell, 2002).

CHAPTER 1

1. David Dunning, "We Are All Confident Idiots," *Pacific Standard*, 2014, https://psmag.com/we-are-all-confident-idiots-56a60eb7febc#.dm3jqn2ds.

2. David Dunning, "The Dunning-Kruger Effect," *Advances in Experimental Social Psychology*, 2011, 247–296, doi:10.1016/b978-0-12-385522-0.00005-6.

3. Oliver Sheldon, Daniel Ames, and David Dunning, "Emotionally Unskilled, Unaware, and Disinterested in Learning More," PsycEXTRA Dataset, doi:10.1037/e527772014-991.

4. Nicolas Slonimsky, *Lexicon of Musical Invective: Critical Assaults on Composers Since Beethoven's Time* (New York: Coleman-Ross, 1965).

5. Albert H. Hastorf and Hadley Cantril, "They Saw a Game: A Case Study," *Journal of Abnormal and Social Psychology* 49, no. 1 (1954): 129.

6. Leon Festinger, Henry W. Riecken, and Stanley Schachter, *When Prophecy Fails* (London: Pinter & Martin Publishers, 2008).

7. "Good Intentions Perverse Incentives," YouTube video, https://www.youtube.com/watch?v=5lIbWtOvRo8.

8. Leana Wen, "Before the Prescription, Ask About Your Doctor's Finances," NPR, December 14, 2013, accessed October 2, 2016, http://www.npr.org/sections/health-shots/2013/12/14/250714833/before-the-prescription-ask -about -your-doctors-finances.

CHAPTER 2

1. "Fact," Merriam-Webster.com, Merriam-Webster, n.d., accessed September 13, 2016, https://www.merriam-webster.com/dictionary/fact.

2. Florin Dolcos, Kevin S. LaBar, and Roberto Cabeza, "Remembering One Year Later: Role of the Amygdala and the Medial Temporal Lobe Memory System in Retrieving Emotional Memories," *Proceedings of the National Academy of Sciences of the United States of America* 102, no. 7 (2005): 2626–2631.

3. Özlem Ayduk and Ethan Kross, "From a Distance: Implications of Spontaneous Self-Distancing for Adaptive Self-Reflection," *Journal of Personality and Social Psychology* 98, no. 5 (2010): 809.

CHAPTER 3

1. Theresa B. Moyers and William R. Miller, "Is Low Therapist Empathy Toxic?," *Psychology of Addictive Behaviors* 27, no. 3 (2013): 878.

2. Noah J. Goldstein, I. Stephanie Vezich, and Jenessa R. Shapiro, "Perceived Perspective Taking: When Others Walk in Our Shoes," *Journal of Personality and Social Psychology* 106, no. 6 (2014): 941.

3. Eytan Bakshy, Solomon Messing, and Lada A. Adamic, "Exposure to Ideologically Diverse News and Opinion on Facebook," *Science* 348, no. 6239 (2015): 1130–1132.

4. Donald A. Redelmeier and Amos Tversky, "Discrepancy Between Medical Decisions for Individual Patients and for Groups," *Preference, Belief, and Similarity* (1990): 887.

CHAPTER 4

1. Emma Bruehlman-Senecal and Ozlem Ayduk, "This Too Shall Pass: Temporal Distance and the Regulation of Emotional Distress," *Journal of Personality and Social Psychology* 108, no. 2 (2015): 356.

2. Lauren Weber, "Bad at Their Jobs, and Loving It," *Wall Street Journal* (web log), May 27, 2013, http://blogs.wsj.com/atwork/2013/03/27/bad-at-their-jobs-and-loving-it/?mod=WSJ_Management_At_Work.

CHAPTER 5

1. Laurence Alison, Emily Alison, Geraldine Noone, Stamatis Elntib, Sara Waring, and Paul Christiansen, "The Efficacy of Rapport-Based Techniques for Minimizing Counter-Interrogation Tactics Amongst a Field Sample of Terrorists," *Psychology, Public Policy, and Law* 20, no. 4 (2014): 421.

CHAPTER 6

1. David Tuller, "Defining an Illness Is Fodder for Debate," *New York Times*, March 7, 2011, accessed October 2, 2016, http://www.nytimes.com/2011/03/08/health/research/08fatigue.html.

2. Herbert J. Klausmeier and Katherine V. Feldman, "Effects of a Definition and a Varying Number of Examples and Non-examples on Concept Attainment," *Journal of Educational Psychology* 67, no. 2 (1975): 174.

3. James M. Clark and Allan Paivio, "Extensions of the Paivio, Yuille, and Madigan (1968) Norms," *Behavior Research Methods, Instruments, & Computers* 36, no. 3 (2004): 371–383.

4. Elliot Aronson, Carrie Fried, and Jeff Stone, "Overcoming Denial and Increasing the Intention to Use Condoms Through the Induction of Hypocrisy," *American Journal of Public Health* 81, no. 12 (1991): 1636–1638.

5. *Monitor*, APA, July 1994.

CHAPTER 7

1. R. G. Nichols and L. A. Stevens, "Listening to People. Reprinted from *Harvard Business Review*, September–October 1957, Number 57507," in Harvard Business Review, *Paths Toward Personal Progress: Leaders Are Made, Not Born* (Cambridge, MA: President and Fellows of Harvard College, 1983); Ralph G. Nichols, "Factors in Listening Comprehension," *Communications Monographs* 15, no. 2 (1948): 154–163.

2. Howard B. Beckman and Richard M. Frankel, "The Effect of Physician Behavior on the Collection of Data," *Annals of Internal Medicine* 101, no. 5 (1984): 692–696, doi:10.7326/0003-4819-101-5-692.

3. M. Kim Marvel, Ronald M. Epstein, Kristine Flowers, and Howard B. Beckman, "Soliciting the Patient's Agenda: Have We Improved?," *Journal of the American Medical Association* 281, no. 3 (1999): 283–287.

4. Lawrence Dyche and Deborah Swiderski, "The Effect of Physician Solicitation Approaches on Ability to Identify Patient Concerns," *Journal of General Internal Medicine* 20, no. 3 (2005): 267–270.

5. James A. Roberts and Meredith E. David. "My Life Has Become a Major Distraction from My Cell Phone: Partner Phubbing and Relationship Satisfaction Among Romantic Partners," *Computers in Human Behavior*, 54 (2016): 134–141.

CHAPTER 8

1. Because of rounding, the percentages only total 99 percent instead of 100 percent.

INDEX

ABOUT THE AUTHOR

Mark Murphy is a *New York Times* bestselling author, contributor to *Forbes*, contributor to LinkedIn, and founder of Leadership IQ, a research and training firm.

Mark is ranked as one of the Top 30 leadership gurus in the world, and some of his most well-known research studies include "Are SMART Goals Dumb?," "Why CEOs Get Fired," "Why New Hires Fail," "High Performers Can Be Less Engaged," and "Don't Expect Layoff Survivors to Be Grateful."

Mark leads one of the world's largest databases of original leadership research, and his work has appeared in the *Wall Street Journal*, the *New York Times, Fortune, Forbes, Bloomberg Businessweek*, and *U.S. News & World Report.* Mark has also appeared on CNN, NPR, CBS *Sunday Morning*, ABC's *20/20*, and the Fox Business Network.

Mark has lectured at the United Nations, Harvard Business School, the Clinton Foundation, Microsoft, Merck, MasterCard, Charles Schwab, Aflac, and hundreds more.

Mark's most recent book was the *New York Times* bestseller *Hundred Percenters: Challenge Your People to Give It Their All and They'll Give You Even More.*

Before that, his book *Hiring for Attitude* was featured in *Fast Company* and the *Wall Street Journal* and was chosen as a top business book by CNBC.

Some of his other books include *HARD Goals: The Science of Getting from Where You Are to Where You Want to Be* and *The Deadly Sins of Employee Retention.*

FOR MORE INFORMATION

For free downloadable resources including quizzes and discussion guides, please visit www.leadershipiq.com/truth.